THE GROUP DYNAMIC FIELD GUIDE

Dear Pam —

Thank you for your kind words — keep meeting needs!

Alan Feirer

THE GROUP DYNAMIC FIELD GUIDE

51 Ideas Leaders Can Use Today

ALAN FEIRER

The Group Dynamic Field Guide

51 Ideas Leaders can Use Today

Group Dynamic Publications
1128 W Jefferson St
Winterset, IA 50273

Ordering Information:
Quantity sales. Special discounts are available on quantity purchases by corporations, associations, and others. For details, contact the publisher at the address above.

First Edition

ISBN-13: 9780692679180 (Group Dynamic Publications)
ISBN-10: 0692679189

Final layout and cover design by Jordan Kuhns Design.
Cover Photograph © 2015 iStock by Preto Perola.

DEDICATION...

My beloved wife, Julie Feirer, who supports, encourages, and challenges me.

My lovely daughter, Mara Feirer, who challenges, encourages, and supports me.

My amazing mother, Sally Wilke, who always made me feel like I could do anything.

Lauren Williams, who was the first person to say "If you write a book, I would *totally* buy it!" Get out your cash, Lauren.

Dr. Art Sunleaf, who was one of my first challengers, supporters, and encouragers.

TABLE OF CONTENTS

FOREWORD

"The last thing the world needs is another book on leadership."
I've said that a lot, in response to the question "When are you writing your first book?"

I fought it for years, but the question comes more frequently now. It's flattering, but I need to get over myself; it's not about me. Rather, it's about a bias toward action and a desire for tools.

So much leadership development and leadership writing is focused on theory, not action. Those books are out there, and it makes sense to check them out to understand the context and rationale of leadership best practices. Some of the best are found in the reference section.

While it's important to dive deep and not insult the capabilities of aspiring and accomplished leaders, it's also important to provide hope, inspiration, and a way to put things into practice, regardless of how much "stuff" a leader has learned. The notions that follow are the ones that people have asked to have in writing for easy reference.

The world and workplace do not wait for leaders to be properly assessed, trained, and "developed." Instead, people end up getting promoted because someone else has left. People take the chair of a committee because it's "their turn." And we've all seen people promoted to leadership because they were good at their job, even though that job and the new job require totally different skill sets.

Leadership is the act of meeting needs. If this is true, and leaders need ideas to put that into action NOW, then the next step is clear: Provide this book for those leaders.

And whether we are just beginning or continuing to explore and develop leaders, we can all turn to this two-word action plan for effective leadership as a touchstone:

MEET NEEDS.

Meeting needs requires curiosity. A leader has to ask, "What's needed?" and then act on it.

Depending on the situation, variations on this question could be...

"What does she need from me?"

"What does this team need right now?"

"What does he/she need to hear to do his/her best work?"

And so on.

The answer a leader comes up with might be 100% right on, but more likely it's just close: 50-80% right on. Still, the resulting actions will be better informed and motivated than actions based on immediate gut reaction.

As you read this book, consider a bias toward **action**. The world moves when we do. Lack of initiative doesn't result in lack of change; it results in decay. It all comes down to "what's needed now."

HOW TO USE THIS BOOK

Here are some suggestions for reading and applying this material, based on your individual needs and available time.

1. Read it beginning to end, but pause to complete each reflection question, and ask a trusted person to share their thoughts on your self-perception.

2. Read just one segment per week, on Sunday, and complete the reflection question. Stay focused on that question during your work throughout the week. On Wednesday afternoon or Thursday morning, ask a trusted person to rate you on that reflection question, then implement their feedback the rest of the week.

3. Rate yourself on all the reflection questions first, then start reading the segments in which you've rated yourself the lowest.

4. Skim the Table of Contents and mark the top 5 segments that pique your curiosity. Read those in one week, one per day. Then, the next week, stay focused on those 5. Repeat the process 9 more times until you've digested the first 50.

Regardless of how you approach it, reflection and discussion with a trusted person are important for embracing the concepts presented.

THE 8 POINT LEADERSHIP MODEL

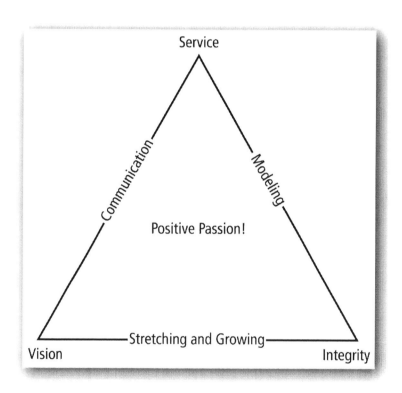

The points represent the three-legged stool of leadership mindsets: Leaders must have a commitment to <u>service</u>, clear <u>vision</u>, and consistent <u>integrity</u>.

The legs connect the mindsets with visible implementation: Leaders master <u>communication</u>, consistently <u>modeling</u> what is expected, and commit to <u>stretching and growing</u>.

In the middle, the pervasive display of <u>passion</u>, expressed in <u>positive</u> ways.

For the very curious, the origin story of the model is in the Afterword. For now, let's have a bias toward action and dig in to Service.

SECTION ONE: SERVICE

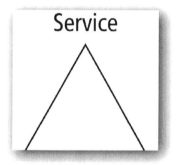

The essence of leadership is service.

The idea that service is essential in the role of leaders is not new. Robert Greenleaf paved the way for opening minds to this concept a few decades ago, and Peter Block did a fine job of refining it by naming it "stewardship". Now, the concept is quite widely accepted.

When approaching any individual, any team, any organization – a good leader asks, "What is needed?" rather than, "What am I supposed to do now to maintain control?"

How many assistant managers, shift supervisors, team leaders and CEOs have ended up in leadership positions as the result of a natural chain of events, without having ever planned for a future in leadership? Many. This often results in a misunderstanding of how to lead. It becomes very easy for someone to become a leader and think, "I'm in charge."

There's nothing inherently wrong with that idea. It's okay to be "in charge". The problem is that it can lead to other assumptions like, "These people had better do what I say. They'd better respect my authority. There's a lot of pressure on me to make sure everyone gets the job done." These thoughts may be true, but they keep the focus on the leader, not the organization and its members (where it should be).

Acting from a place of serving and meeting needs just plain works, but it is also nuanced, which is why we can't stop here. How do we accurately determine what is needed? How do we execute? How do we balance the system along with its politics, traditions, and human relations?

We can't stop with, "A leader serves." But, it is where we start. Instead of thinking, "I've done my share," think, "What more can be done?"

"...be authentic, be vulnerable, be present, be accepting, and be useful. And by useful I mean, be servants." – James Autry

Rate yourself – and ask others to rate you – on this:

When approaching a situation, I actively seek to find out what is needed of me, rather than what I can do to maintain control.

(low)   1   2   3   4   5   (high)

Self-perception:

_____

_____

_____

Feedback from others:

_____

_____

_____

_____

_____

Reading 1

● ● ●

MEET NEEDS

I ate in a London pub with a group once, and the server made a mistake when calculating the bill. Unfortunately, he didn't believe us, and the ensuing argument kept escalating.

Confession: I got a little... um... animated.

He was in the wrong (I have witnesses), but now he had a service issue with an obviously upset customer (me), so he pulled out the "last resort" at his disposal:

"What do you want me to do, exactly?"

Great question! Hearing this calmed me down and gave me the chance to stop listing facts, numbers, and the order of events, and simply say:

"Acknowledge that Daniel has paid, and stop trying to charge him twice."

The server then proceeded to do a lot of slamming around of change and drawers, and told us never to come back, but Daniel was spared being double-charged.

This story isn't about leadership directly, but it can be adapted to illustrate an important instruction:

At points of exasperation, when you're tempted to escalate or argue, why not stop and ask: "What do you need that you're not getting?"

Answers to this question could surprise you, help you, and allow you to serve your follower(s) with less tension and greater speed (as long as you are sincere when asking).

Also – and this is big – it can reinforce the connection between you and your team. Remember, you are seeking the chance to MEET NEEDS, which is your ultimate responsibility as a leader.

Real-world answers to this question that I have personally heard, or heard about:

"Respect from you."

"Water."

"A more comfortable chair."

"...for Brenda to be fired."

"More light."

"...for people to stop taking my equipment bag without asking."

Once you have an answer, you can move forward. Sometimes you can satisfy a reasonable request; sometimes the answer is real, but unrelated to the original topic; sometimes the request is laughably unreasonable (you CAN'T fire someone at someone else's request – that doesn't actually meet the needs of the organization, usually).

Even if you can't immediately act on the answer, you've gotten to the bottom of things to a greater extent, shown concern for needs, slowed things down, and you're closer to solving the problem and getting back to work.

Rate yourself – and ask others to rate you – on this:

When I sense conflict or tension, I ask my team variations of "What do you need that you are not getting?"

(low)   1   2   3   4   5   (high)

Self-perception:

_____

_____

_____

Feedback from others:

_____

_____

_____

_____

Reading 2

● ● ●

ADDRESS THIS COMMON OBSTACLE

Dr. Tim Lautzenheiser, a highly regarded, internationally known educator, coined this concept: The Four Levels of Maturity.

The Four Levels of Maturity is an easy-to-grasp simplification of some developmental psychology concepts.

Combining this way of looking at maturity with the concepts in *Leadership and Self-Deception* (from The Arbinger Institute) has proven to be a very effective way to help people learn how to tolerate other people.

It's also a great tool for personal growth and better leadership.

LEVEL I: SELFISH ("WHAT'S IN IT FOR ME?")

Behaviors on this level are focused entirely on gratification. Examples of this behavior include ignoring office housekeeping tasks, being late, answering your cell phone or texting in the middle of a conversation, not flushing a public toilet because you don't feel like touching the handle, etc. These are all selfish behaviors, executed with little regard for the impact they may have on others.

LEVEL II: INDEPENDENT ("I'LL DO MY JOB – BUT THAT'S IT.")

This level is most dangerous, because when we behave at this level, we *think* we're a team player, because we're technically following the rules. The mindset here is, "I've taken care of all my stuff. It doesn't matter to me if you have done the same. None of my business." Behaviors at this level include cleaning your own dishes (but ignoring your coworkers'), but walking past others', being on time, but not offering a ride to someone else who might also be late, finishing your work ahead of schedule, but failing to offer help to those who are a bit behind – "Not my problem, not my fault."

The first two levels are both self-centered, with no real regard for "team" or other people in the world.

If you're familiar with *Leadership and Self-Deception*, those levels are referred to as acting "in the box." You may hear me also refer to these two levels as acting "below the line." You don't want to be there.

LEVEL III: COOPERATIVE (BEING EMPATHETIC AND EFFECTIVE)

Behaviors at this level include working together according to everyone's strengths, weaknesses and capabilities, to get things done for the team, or the world at large. "I'll pick up this letter, if you hold the door for me" or "I'll staple the cover pages to the reports if you run them up to Finance." Most successful organizations see these behaviors relatively frequently from their team members, and nearly all the time from their leaders. This is where we land when we're being easy to work with. But – the most effective leaders and team members cannot rest at this level, because there will always be people acting at levels one and two "below the line".

LEVEL IV: GIVING (ACTIVELY FINDING AND MEETING NEEDS)

Acting at this level means you have made a consistent commitment to meeting the needs of others, and of the group, in order to get things done. It isn't about being a pushover, or enabling selfish behaviors in others, but an acknowledgment that many people have habitual behaviors at levels one and two.

If you've read *Leadership and Self-Deception*, you really grow to understand this idea:

When people are "below the line," or acting at levels one and two, there is absolutely no patient way to get them to grow up and act at levels three and four.

While there is no *efficient* way to do this, there is an *effective* way – by constantly acting "above the line". That is, constantly demonstrate behaviors at levels three and four.

Rate yourself – and ask others to rate you – on this:

I actively work to operate within maturity Levels III and IV, and encourage others to do so as well.

(low)   1   2   3   4   5   (high)

Self-perception:

_____

_____

_____

Feedback from others:

_____

_____

_____

_____

_____

Reading 3

● ● ●

LISTEN MORE. TALK LESS. PAUSE AND LEARN.

Leaders often know what the needs are in a situation, and dictate them with authority. While the leader is often correct about the direction, engagement can suffer without more buy-in; asking questions that help others discover the same needs can help.

Even when you know what is needed, consider expanding your own understanding, helping others buy in and be a part of the process by asking questions similar to these:

Based on what you know, what do you think we should do next? Is this situation similar to anything you've ever dealt with before? Any thoughts on our next move, based on that? If you were in my shoes, what would you suggest we do now? When we look at all the factors, do you see a clear option or two we should consider? If I left for a week, and put you in charge of this, what would you do?

For example, it's become clear that Friday afternoon meetings are less effective than the Wednesday late morning meetings. If you have a team member that you need to solidify a relationship with, or who feels like s/he isn't always "heard," consider asking that person "If you were in charge of scheduling these meetings, would you leave them on Friday, or just have them all on Wednesday?"

The answer will likely be the solution you've considered, so now you've turned them into a trusted team member by adopting their idea. And if the answer is different, you'll learn something. For example, they may come back with "Wednesday seems like the better idea, because those always go better, but sometimes we get new TPS reports on Thursday, so a Friday meeting makes more sense those weeks. What if we put them late Thursday, though?"

In *Winning*, GE's Jack Welch points out that listening more and talking less helps to meet needs:

> **"Obviously, some people have better ideas than others; some people are smarter or more experienced or more creative. But, everyone should be heard and respected. They want it, and you need it."**

Two other books really pound this home, too. In Ury's *The Power of a Positive No*, he explains that his understanding of the "other" was critical to his success as a hostage negotiator.

Even more potent is the aforementioned *Leadership and Self-Deception*, which I'd call one of the most influential leadership books I've ever read.

Again, the common theme in these books is that leaders ought to listen more, talk less, pause and learn. Please, heed their advice.

Rate yourself – and ask others to rate you – on this:

I make time to question others about their viewpoints, and listen to their ideas, concerns, and opinions.

(low)   1   2   3   4   5   (high)

Self-perception:

_____

_____

_____

Feedback from others:

_____

_____

_____

_____

_____

Reading 4

● ● ●

KNOW ROLE POWER V. RELATIONSHIP POWER

I saw a Disney cast member holler at a child once - and it was perfectly appropriate.

Disney cast members are highly trained in many ways. You likely know of their magical customer service and commitment to staying in character. They also make sure the parks run smoothly, but the order in which all of these commitments play out is not at all random.

Disney gives all staff (cast) a clear priority order of their Basics, or Keys:

1. Safety
2. Courtesy
3. Show
4. Efficiency

If everything is going well – no safety issues, everyone is cooperating, and there are no challenges to staying "in character," then cast members are free to do whatever is most efficient to get things moving quickly for guests, whether it's a line, or food, or a character interaction.

However, they will let efficiency slide to keep the "show" intact – to stay in character. If you eat at the 50s Prime Time Cafe, part of the show is that they bring you nothing unless you say "please". For everything. I asked for "Diet Coke, and water, please" and she brought me only the water. "Still waiting for that Diet Coke," I said a few times, until I realized that I had never paired "Diet Coke" with "please". Once I did, there it was. Our server came around and hovered a lot to give me the opportunity - totally inefficient, but part of the show, and my daughter loved it.

The show may slide for the sake of courtesy. The cast at The Haunted Mansion is glum and stern, and a bit creepy. The ride itself isn't that scary, and when a small child started crying in line, a cast member broke character, took the child aside, sat on the curb with her, and explained – you may even say spoiled – every single effect and visual of the attraction. The cast member smiled, encouraged, and patiently explained. Courtesy trumps show.

On the Winnie the Pooh attraction, a toddler ahead of me worked his way out from under the lap bar in his Hunny Pot and started to stand on the seat, so quickly that there was no time to politely modify his behavior.

"HEY! SIT DOWN! SIT DOWN *NOW*!!!" hollered the cast member - out of character, not in show, not efficient (she stopped letting people on the attraction in those moments), and certainly not courteous.

The toddler obeyed, and we were all shaken up, but it made perfect sense. Safety is huge at Disney - and should be for you, too. A safe culture frees people from fear.

If you've heard me talk about giving up Role power for Relationship power, you know that Role power is absolutely required when safety is in jeopardy. When that's the only time it's invoked, it's pretty powerful.

Another thing that's powerful? A clear priority of what you need to be most mindful of in any given situation. Watch for Safety, Courtesy, Show, and Efficiency as you go about your day or execute your own work. Even though we're not running Disney World, we can learn from the best and apply those lessons in *our* world.

Rate yourself – and ask others to rate you – on this:

I remain alert and attentive to what my first priority is day-to-day. Should I be attending to one priority (efficiency) and a major concern arises (safety), I quickly shift direction to take care of that need.

(low)   1   2   3   4   5   (high)

Self-perception:

_____

_____

_____

Feedback from others:

_____

_____

_____

_____

_____

Reading 5

● ● ●

ASK THIS IMPORTANT QUESTION

If the two-word action plan for leadership is "meet needs," then you have frequent opportunities to be very explicit about that mission by taking just three seconds to ask some variation of:

"Is there anything I can do to help you with that?"

Variations to get you started:

"May I show you how?"

"Would you like help?"

"Should we come up with a system?"

"What if I send you a reminder?"

"What do you need to make sure that happens?"

If any command, criticism, new instruction, behavior-outcome statement (we'll cover this in reading 16), or problem identification is immediately followed by this willingness to help, you will provide safety and assistance for those you serve.

Some critics may argue that helping people will only make them less capable of showing initiative on their own, but I disagree. Working with your people to solve problems, and teaching them to do so, will lead to greater independence and better relationships in the future. They will only show more individual initiative when you show them how to do so.

If you're correcting punctuality issues, offer a reminder alert. If you're addressing sloppy work, offer a model – or to proofread a rough draft. If disrespectful body language in meetings is the issue, offer a code word or gesture to remind them they're falling back into old habits.

Try this for a couple weeks, and see what happens. "Is there anything I can do to help you with that?" Use it cautiously, however; if the task is very simple, or if you have the wrong tone, this could come across sarcastically.

Rate yourself – and ask others to rate you – on this:

I intentionally and frequently ask my team variations of, "What can I do to help you with that?" especially after making a request or providing critical feedback.

(low)   1   2   3   4   5   (high)

Self-perception:

Feedback from others:

SECTION TWO: VISION

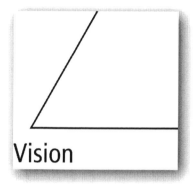

Vision

Effective leaders must have vision. Not just in the "creatively imagined future" way, but also in the way of "I have an accurate assessment of the way things are right now."

Leaders must (in the words of those wise men, Kouzes and Posner) "inspire a shared vision". Without knowing what the goals are, folks are rarely motivated. It's the "purpose" in the trifecta of Dan Pink's *Drive*: Autonomy, Mastery and Purpose.

While much is often made of that "creatively imagined future" form of vision, some leaders neglect the need to accurately read the "here and now".

Motivation toward the shared vision can erode when the leader is out of touch with the current state of affairs; an overly optimistic leader can turn people off if there are ignored dysfunctions. Similarly, an overly pessimistic leader can bring down morale.

In developing the "future" sense of vision, many organizational leaders are already familiar with "SWOT" activities — these are good, and make sense.

In developing the "here and now" sense of vision, wise leaders will use assessments, 360's, focus groups, or other tools to sharpen their awareness.

It's wise to use caution, though; over-analysis can stand in the way of getting the day-to-day work done. Do what you need to do, but nothing more. The "Three Things" activity I'll share next is one way to engage others in this vision development, and it can build a bridge between the two.

Where are you going? Whether it's simple or complex, make sure there's an answer to that question.

> **"The best coaches know what the end result looks like ... if you don't know what the end result looks like, you can't get there." – Vince Lombardi**

Rate yourself – and ask others to rate you – on this:

I can accurately describe both A) the ideal state of our group and B) the exact current state of our group.

(low)   1   2   3   4   5   (high)

Self-perception:

_____

_____

_____

Feedback from others:

_____

_____

_____

_____

Reading 6

● ● ●

LEARN TO BE VISIONARY

Let's make this concept easier, more concrete, more actionable, and more "learnable," with the Three Things activity. This is something I learned and adapted from Dr. Tim Lautzenheiser.

STEP ONE – Make two lists, of three items each:

1) List three words or phrases that describe your organization as it *is now*, <u>but you wish were not true</u>.

2) List three words or phrases you *wish* would describe your organization, but that <u>aren't true now</u>.

For example, here were my responses in an organization I was once associated with:

1. pessimistic, stressed people, culture of fear [current reality – not desirable]
2. forward-thinking, celebratory, high-achieving [ideal reality – what's desired]

STEP TWO – Look in the mirror, and ask, "Which of these six words or phrases describe ME?"

Then write them down.

For example: Honestly, I was pessimistic, and one of the stressed people, but I was also forward-thinking.

STEP THREE – Set a goal for yourself to either...

1) Eliminate one of the undesirables, or 2) take on one of the desirables.

For example: I could have made a goal for myself to cease any pessimistic behaviors — to never again say anything about impending trouble, or the gloom of the current state.

By doing so, you become part of the solution, not part of the problem.

Also, you've taken a step in developing your own concept of **vision** — the ability to honestly assess the current state, and imaginatively picture the ideal state.

What if everyone in your business/organization/team did this exercise?

Rate yourself – and ask others to rate you – on this:

Based on where my team is right now, and where I know they need to be, I take active measures to get us from point A to point B.

(low)   1   2   3   4   5   (high)

Self-perception:

_____

_____

_____

Feedback from others:

_____

_____

_____

_____

Reading 7

• • •

KNOW THE VALUE IN RUBRICS

We all need a starting point for discussions about vision, direction, prioritization, and hiring. That's precisely why leaders love rubrics (scoring tools). Simple rubrics are easy to create and implement, and help make things clear.

Consider using a scale of 1 to 3, or 1 to 5, to keep them simple.

Rubric Example 1

You're considering candidates for a position, and they're all good.

Start by listing your values, or other traits you're looking for, in one column on a spreadsheet.

Put the names of the candidates at the top. Then, rate them all on a scale of 1 to 5 for each value or desired trait.

You'll quickly see who scores the highest, or the lowest, and can use that as a starting point.

Rubric Example 2

Your team is overwhelmed.

Due to this, you've experienced "task creep," or perhaps you've taken on some exciting new projects.

Rate all the tasks on a scale of 1 to 3.

List the tasks/projects on the top row. And in the left column, list these criteria:

- Value to Staff/Employees (makes this a great place to work)
- Value to Customers (makes you the provider of choice)
- Value to Owners/Shareholders (makes money)

Looking at your projects this way will help you prioritize where to put your efforts first.

And, if something reveals itself as not urgent, it's a good time to delegate that task back to your team – but make sure they understand the task's priority level.

Rubric Example 3

Feeling a lack of direction? Every day, I apply a rubric to my to-do list.

I mark items with an "A" if they must be done today, "B" if they ought to be done this week, and "C" if they require attention, but aren't that urgent.

Overwhelmed? Create a rubric.

Rate yourself – and ask others to rate you – on this:

I make use of simple rubrics to help myself, and my team, get clarity of direction when needed.

(low)   1   2   3   4   5   (high)

Self-perception:

_____

_____

_____

Feedback from others:

_____

_____

_____

_____

_____

Reading 8

● ● ●

ATTEND TO ACTION PLANS

Have you ever been part of a strategic planning initiative that resulted in a long document, with a 3-year timeline, and several action plans?

Many times, these action plans and initiatives involve projects that go above and beyond the day-to-day work of an organization.

And, particularly if it's a volunteer-driven group, it's common that as much as 80% of those plans stay on the shelf and never get put into action.

As a leader, what can you do when you realize this has happened?

Break out those abandoned plans, gather two other people to create a committee of three, and put them in priority order.

Once prioritized, "triage" them – decide which are best to abandon, and which are best to renew efforts toward. It's okay to have a "middle" pile of "maybes."

I recommend picking just one or two to renew efforts on. When you've picked them, include action elements as a part of your regular agenda, and get them done.

Also, formalize your decision to abandon the ones you're leaving behind; this shows the team that it's okay to change course, and it's better to be deliberate about it.

Going forward, what can you do to keep this kind of thing from happening?

From the beginning, make sure each action plan has an owner, and some deadlines for its tasks.

During every meeting, spend 15 seconds on each plan – just ask the owner for a one-color status update:

- **Green – it's on track to meet the deadline.**
- **Yellow – it's at risk of falling behind.**
- **Red – it is behind.**

If it's yellow or red, ask the owner "what help do you need from anyone here?"

Then, act on the answer.

Rate yourself – and ask others to rate you – on this:

To move along planned initiatives, I work with my team to prioritize, toss out, assign ownership and deadlines, and regularly check in on them.

(low)   1   2   3   4   5   (high)

Self-perception:

_____

_____

_____

Feedback from others:

_____

_____

_____

_____

Reading 9

● ● ●

DECIDE: STOP, START, CONTINUE

Another quick way to move forward is to do a simple "Start, Stop, Continue." Do this: put up 3 pieces of chart paper, one for each word.

Have on hand:

- calendar of events, activities, recurring projects
- a list of current projects or initiatives
- job descriptions or lists of daily activities and tasks

As you comb through those lists, you can put them on the "stop" or "continue" sheet — most will end up in the "continue" category.

Discuss any possible "stop" nominations. Most organizations have some dead weight there somewhere, in terms of low-ROI (return on investment) activities.

For example, you could stop…

- a social media campaign around a service with a low profit margin.
- a policy requiring people to avoid leaving for lunch between noon and 1, because there is next to no foot traffic during that time anyway.
- a beautification project for the front of the property when there is a 90% chance you're about to move to a new space.

Then, as your discussions unfold, there will inevitably be times when someone says, "Well, you know what we *could* do..."

At that point, you have new ideas to put on the "start" sheet. That way, ideas for new initiatives or ways of doing things arise organically, and not as a result of freewheeling brainstorming.

For example, you could start...

- to move most marketing efforts to your most unique and/or high margin service.
- Closing your doors from 12:30 to 1:00 to allow staff to eat together. (The shoe repair shop that I use has this policy. It's admirable.)

There's a time and a place for all-out strategic planning.

But, just doing a "Stop, Start, Continue" on any scale (consider doing one for your own day-to-day work) can provide renewed focus.

Rate yourself – and ask others to rate you – on this:

When all-out strategic planning can be spared, I use a simple "Stop, Start, Continue" to keep myself, and team, on track.

(low)   1   2   3   4   5   (high)

Self-perception:

_____

_____

_____

Feedback from others:

_____

_____

_____

_____

_____

Reading 10

● ● ●

WRITE EFFECTIVE GOALS AND HELP OTHERS TO DO SO

You don't have to look too far to find information on how to write SMART goals. But sometimes, that 5-step rubric can intimidate or push us in the wrong direction.

Another great way to write effective goals is to ensure that just two important elements are included:

1. Specific actions.
2. Timelines and/or deadlines.

For example, let's say I've been grumpy, and have been missing deadlines. I'd better change!

Three approaches – in order of effectiveness:

Avoid: "I'm going to be less casual about deadlines, and more positive about our work."

Better: "This month, I'm going to get the TPS reports in on Thursday, and start saying more positive things about my team."

Best: "On Thursdays, I will turn my TPS reports in 1 hour early. This trigger will remind me to find a positive comment to share with at least two people. I will do this each week for a month, then come up with a new goal to make a habit of."

It's much easier for others to hold you accountable to the third approach. And, the use of triggers can really help.

Rate yourself – and ask others to rate you – on this:

*My goals are specific, and include timelines or deadlines to keep me accountable. *Bonus points for helping your team set goals this way, too. ***

(low)   1   2   3   4   5   (high)

Self-perception:

_____

_____

_____

Feedback from others:

_____

_____

_____

_____

SECTION THREE: INTEGRITY

Integrity

Does it go without saying that leaders must have integrity? Maybe it just can't be said enough.

A manager once told me about having to let a seemingly great hire go. Seeing my surprise, she looked me in the eye and said, "He didn't walk the talk."

The folks at Iowa's Character Counts use a great correlation:

If having character in your personal life — moral character — can be called being your "best self," then having character in the workplace — performance character — can be termed "best work".

Consistency in decision-making and the way people are treated builds credibility and develops relationships. The constant practice of staying mature in the moment, and treating others with dignity, furthers those relationships.

Great reads on this topic include *Credibility* and *Leadership and Self-Deception*.

"Leadership is serious meddling in other people's lives" – Max DePree

Rate yourself – and ask others to rate you – on this:

I have high moral standards, and my actions are consistent with those values.

(low)   1   2   3   4   5   (high)

Self-perception:

_____

_____

_____

Feedback from others:

_____

_____

_____

_____

Reading 11

DO WHAT YOU SAY YOU WILL DO

In their research on Characteristics of Admired Leaders, Kouzes and Posner found this: Far and away, the most desired characteristics of leaders are (in this order):

Honest, Forward-Looking, Inspiring, and Competent.

It's fascinating that both "inspiring" AND "competent" are on the list together, as frequently a person in a leadership role demonstrates one characteristic but not the other.

What really stands out is that out of all the things a leader can be, HONEST is at the top of the list.

We can't always subject ourselves to polygraph tests, so how do we "prove" that we are honest?

Here's how: Do what you say you will do (DWYSYWD).

Do you expect people to be fully engaged in meetings? Then YOU had best never look at your phone during a meeting, and keep your laptop closed.

Do you expect people to put customers ahead of routine tasks? Then, YOU need to allow your team members to interrupt your routine tasks.

Do you expect employees to park away from the building? You guessed it — YOU must park the furthest away.

I had the chance to visit a corporate headquarters once. This particular company had some bad word-of-mouth in terms of having a toxic culture.

When I arrived, I saw that there was a large luxury automobile parked in the very front – in the middle of a fire lane, with one wheel up on the curb, and blocking the wheelchair ramp.

Turned out it belonged to the CEO, and when I learned that, it all made sense.

Do what you say you will do, and actively demonstrate your core values.

Rate yourself – and ask others to rate you – on this:

I follow through on what I promise to deliver; I Do What I Say I Will Do.

(low)   1   2   3   4   5   (high)

Self-perception:

_____

_____

_____

Feedback from others:

_____

_____

_____

_____

_____

Reading 12

● ● ●

ACTIVELY DEMONSTRATE YOUR CORE VALUES

Once, on a two-hour flight, the man sitting to my left kept accidentally jabbing me with his elbow – repeatedly.

I'm empathetic; he was in the middle seat. Still, there are "rules," and he was often in my space. With his elbow, with his newspaper, and with his leg and feet. He was a textbook example of the self-centered, inconsiderate plane passenger.

Eventually, he put the paper away, and pulled out a notebook. I confess, I peeked.

He was working on his personal values. No kidding – at the top of the page he was studying, and writing notes on, his guiding value:

"Love my neighbor as myself."

As examples and goals, he had many lofty things written down, like "volunteer at the homeless shelter downtown." His intentions were clear, and good, but his current product?

Inconsiderate foot, leg, and elbow contact. I wanted to chime in and say, "I've got a GREAT idea on how you could show courtesy to your neighbor." But that would be level two on the Maturity scale, at best, so I just huddled closer to the window.

Does your team have "core values?" Probably. But – do you *live* them? The best way to answer that question is to totally define what they look like in terms of work product in these three areas:

1. Personal work
2. Team work
3. Customer-facing work

For example, a Group Dynamic value is "Responsive and Timely." How does that look, when we're at our best?

1. I answer all email and phone communication within 24 hours at most – ideally four hours.
2. My employee and I set deadlines and meet them for each other.
3. When a client has a question, I work to answer it after asking more questions to get to the root of things.

Pick any value, and come up with work-product examples in those three areas, then give (and seek) feedback on how well they are executed.

Push yourself to set values, then define them, and invoke them on a regular basis. It's worth it.

Rate yourself – and ask others to rate you – on this:

My words and actions demonstrate my organization's core values.

(low)   1   2   3   4   5   (high)

Self-perception:

_____

_____

_____

Feedback from others:

_____

_____

_____

_____

_____

Reading 13

AVOID STUPID RULES

A fellow consultant and I once worked with a small services firm that had some retention and engagement problems.

At first, everything seemed in place – the people were good; the quality of their work was sound; the CEO and leadership team cared about their folks. But, looking closer, there were some misguided notions in play that made us scratch our heads.

They had a couple of odd policies:

1. In order to save energy, all overhead lights were off, and only cubicle task lamps were used when needed.
2. In order to preserve professionalism, all employees were to wear suits every day, even though no clients ever came to the place of business.

So, their people came to work each day dressed to the nines, and walked around in the dark, with small directional task lamps dotting the cubicle landscape. And, most of their days were spent working alone.

These well-intentioned policies (note that they did have a rationale) worked against the relationship the organization had with each employee, and actually contributed to the lack of engagement.

This organization even prided itself on the many outings and social opportunities it created for its staff. Because they thought they were doing enough, a few poorly thought out rules worked against their stated values.

And that's the problem; when the policies fail to match the mission or norms of the organization, it results in confusion, at best, or a lack of integrity, at worst.

Eliminate stupid rules, perhaps those you don't follow yourself, and ensure that work and policies reflect your values.

Rate yourself – and ask others to rate you – on this:

I evaluate the rules my team follow, and work to adjust them if they are unfit to reflect our values.

(low)   1   2   3   4   5   (high)

Self-perception:

_____

_____

_____

Feedback from others:

_____

_____

_____

_____

Reading 14

●　●　●

ASK: HOW DOES THAT MAKE YOU FEEL?

At the Disney Institute, participants are challenged to think about how their decisions as leaders or team members make others feel. That seemed basic to me, even insulting, until they pushed us to take a closer look.

Most of us think about how big things make people feel — we're sensitive during that "crucial conversation," we make decent small talk when we can tell that it makes others more comfortable, etc.

BUT – what about little things? Especially routine things?

On small matters, do you turn your full attention to someone, or do you multitask?

Is receiving an email response from you a pleasant experience?

Do you force people to work with your systems, or do you bend to match the idiosyncrasies of others?

As I listened, I still maintained that paying attention to the feelings of others was a strength of mine; after all, I train people on this stuff!

As we all talked to each other, however, I was challenged on a few things:

Does your proposal and acceptance process leave people feeling glad to work with you, or do you make it a routine chore?

When you invoice and collect, do you make it comfortable, or do you seem like "just anyone"?

And, this:

What parts of your routine, your relationships, your teamwork, have you never, ever given any thought to, in terms of "How does this make them feel?"

This really challenged me.

I went down to Disney just a few weeks later, and noticed some things:

A bell services staff person took a silly request for a spare charging cord extremely seriously.

A waiter sensed that something was wrong with my dish and replaced it before I could awkwardly complain.

I also recalled the time I was hot, and tired, and got snarky when I was asked if I needed anything at a drink cart at one of the Disney Parks. I said, "Yeah – you got any overpriced soft drinks?"

Without skipping a beat, that server made me feel awesome. She said "Sure! Want one for free, though?"

What? Really?

"Okay..." I was wary, but she had my attention.

"Order it in Whale."

"Whale?"

"Yeah, like Dory in *Finding Nemo.*"

I did it. I smiled. I got a free Diet Coke, and since I played ball so nicely, they even offered me a free ice cream bar.

Here's the thing; all these examples require no special skills, just habits of thoughtfulness. And they can make a BIG difference in the engagement of those around you.

Improve your effectiveness by paying attention to how everything, big or small, makes people feel.

Rate yourself – and ask others to rate you – on this:

I am attentive to how people feel when interacting with me, even on small-scale, or mundane work.

(low)   1   2   3   4   5   (high)

Self-perception:

_____

_____

_____

Feedback from others:

_____

_____

_____

_____

Reading 15

● ● ●

BEWARE THE SUCCESS DECEPTION

Some of the best teachers I know are people who struggled through school. Some of the weakest teachers I know, conversely, experienced a lot of success. Adversity strengthens us, and success can fool us.

I used to be a band director. In my first of three band jobs, things didn't start out very well, but after about three years, I "figured it out," developed a system, and things worked for that group of 26.

Then, I moved to a new school, and tried the same system for a group of 118. Again, things didn't go very well at first, but after three years, I "figured it out," developed a new system, and things worked for that group.

Then, I moved to a new place, tried the same system… You know where this leads, right? When a leader experiences success, two deceptions occur:

1) This system works! Therefore, it will work everywhere. I've got it all figured out!

2) My approach to people works! Everyone should act like I do, then they will also be successful!

Leaders deluded by this false sense of success are dangerous, because their [justifiable] self-confidence prevents them from entering a mode of self-improvement.

I was in this mode (the wrong one) under my second boss, who told me years later "Man, you couldn't tell that guy (young Alan) *anything!*"

Success deception causes two big problems:

1. Stagnating development, and
2. Lack of appreciation of different approaches from others, leading to judgment, or lack of trust.

"Pride goeth before a fall," right? Enjoy success, but beware of its deceptions. If there is a sweet spot when it comes to personal development, it's this: "I know I don't know it all, but I'm open to learning more." The most successful leaders embrace this.

Do you suffer from the Success Deception? Ask your boss, your highest performing team member, and your best friend. They'll let you know.

Rate yourself – and ask others to rate you – on this:

I remain open, conscious, and aware of my methods. I never rely on them for an assumed future success.

(low)   1   2   3   4   5   (high)

Self-perception:

_____

_____

_____

Feedback from others:

_____

_____

_____

_____

SECTION FOUR: COMMUNICATION

If there's one skill that leaders must master and habitually improve above all, it's communication.

So many dysfunctions, productivity concerns, drama, misunderstandings, and performance failures can be traced directly to communication missteps.

It's tough to summarize this one, but here's an attempt:

Communication goes out, and it comes in. To keep both channels flowing freely:

Communicate "out" with practiced skill:

- Write well.
- Speak clearly and specifically [with solid presentation skills].
- Ensure that your body language is consistent with your message.

Communicate "in" with conscious deliberation:

- Read carefully.
- Listen actively [with verbal, physical, and visual affirmation].
- Be mindful of the tone, body language, and personality style of the speaker.

"The only way to lead when you don't have control is to lead through the power of your relationships." – Margaret Wheatley

Rate yourself – and ask others to rate you – on these:

I listen well, with total focus on the speaker.

(low)   1   2   3   4   5   (high)

I speak well, clearly, specifically, in a way that leaves no question what I meant and that shows total respect to the person listening.

(low)   1   2   3   4   5   (high)

When helping or correcting someone, I address a person's specific actions, not his or her attitude.

(low)   1   2   3   4   5   (high)

Self-perception:

_____

_____

Feedback from others:

_____

_____

_____

_____

Reading 16

● ● ●

BE SPECIFIC BY USING THE BEHAVIOR-OUTCOME STATEMENT

When addressing anything, be specific. Most importantly, make it be about the behavior, and the outcome. The outcome is important because it answers the question "Why?"

Brain research and common sense teach us that people are more willing to buy into something if they know the reasons why. Instead of a long explanation, this can be accomplished quickly and casually by mentioning the outcome.

Being specific is important because it reduces the likelihood of misinterpretation. We often know exactly what we need, but because the person we are talking to isn't psychic, we have to spell it out.

Talking about behavior, rather than general mood, or mindset, or attitude, keeps it real. Also, if it is something negative, this keeps it from being too personal.

So, when addressing things, *be specific*, state the behavior, and state the outcome. We call this the **behavior-outcome statement**. In each pair of examples, the second one is more specific and focuses on behavior and outcome.

[weak] Kate, your attitude sucks this week.

[strong] Kate, when you unleash a heavy sigh after everything that Bill says, it has a negative impact on the progress of the whole group.

[weak] Tim, you're so awesome!

[strong] Tim, when you greet everyone who comes to the door with that sincere look in your eyes and that smile on your face, people are glad they came here. That's good for us.

[weak] Isaac, you don't really seem to care about getting here on time, and I'm getting sick of it.

[strong] Isaac, when you show up late, it keeps other people guessing about when you'll get here and we really aren't able to get down to work until that uncertainty is resolved.

[weak] Joan, great! You're finally showing some commitment get here on time. Thank God.

[strong] Joan, your renewed commitment to being here on time is so helpful to the team. We can get down to business so much more quickly and get to lunch earlier. Thanks.

Speaking specifically, and in terms of behavior and outcome, takes a bit more mental energy, and even some planning ahead.

Making it a habit will make you more effective and increase the buy-in of those you work with. Let's take a look at another scenario:

"Hey Tom, if you could get some of those account reviews done by Thursday, that'd be great."

Sometimes, to sound "nice," we make requests like the one above: casual (that's a good thing), general (bad thing), with a deadline (good thing), but without a specific request (bad thing) or way to measure (very bad thing).

The result can descend into icky-ness. You can picture it…

Tom's boss, Jill, really wants 10 (out of 20 total) done by Friday so she can jump on them right away Monday. She just said to do it by Thursday because she thought that by being vague, they might get done late. She assumes that Tom knows that she wants to take action on these by the end of the month, which is two weeks away. 'If I were in Tom's shoes,' Jill reasons, 'I'd know that I ought to have half of them done.'

Thursday comes, Jill's afraid to ask, Tom doesn't really volunteer anything.

Friday arrives, and Jill asks Tom, "So, I was wondering if, um, you got any of those account reviews done?"

Tom: "Well, yeah, I did two."

"Two!?!?!?"

"Yeah."

"But, but, but…" Jill sputters. She's very very frustrated now. "But I asked so nicely!!!"

Tom is put off by Jill's sudden passive-aggressive obvious frustration. Tension ensues. And endures.

How can we still sound nice (good thing), casual (good thing), and offer a deadline (good thing), and get better results (very good thing)?

By being specific and making a request. Great phrase for that request: "Will you please…?" This still gives people a choice, theoretically, but you won't find a "no" very often.

A better scenario:

"Hey, Tom, we need to get 20 accounts reviewed before next month hits. **Will you please** make time to get 10 account reviews done by Friday?"

"Yikes- ten? Well, alright."

"Need anything from me to help make it happen?"

"Well, since you asked…. will you pick the ten?"

"Sure."

Can you picture that? Sure! It's all still casual, nice, with a deadline, but with two little additions – specificity, and a request. With a bonus "Is there anything you need from me?" thrown in for an extra measure of support.

Kindly, casually, make specific (very specific) requests. See what happens.

Rate yourself – and ask others to rate you – on this:

When addressing behavior (good or bad), and making requests, I communicate with specificity, and always state an outcome.

(low)   1   2   3   4   5   (high)

Self-perception:

_____

_____

_____

Feedback from others:

_____

_____

_____

_____

Reading 17

CREATE CLARITY

Few things are more energizing than leaving a productive meeting with your team, set ablaze with fresh ideas that will set the wheels in motion. You're ready to go. Your team is ready to go. You've established goals and are ready to tackle the world.

It's a great feeling. Until something, somewhere gets a little hazy.

Clarity, a close cousin to specificity, is a valuable follow-through quality that can easily get lost in a drive of enthusiasm. Clarity ensures that everyone is on the same page. While specificity identifies important information (like who is doing what and when it's due), clarity ensures all of the questions are answered before anyone even gets started.

Clarity especially falls victim to team-wide meetings when everyone seems like they're in sync. Once the group thinks everyone understands the situation and expectations involved, a false sense of clarity abounds and no one asks clarifying questions (either because they think they already know the answer, or worse, they think they're the only one who doesn't understand and don't ask out of fear).

So how can you avoid falling into a haze of uncertainty? ***Follow up.***

After the meeting has concluded, make sure notes or minutes with action items go out within 24 hours if possible. Encourage team members to respond with questions, additions or changes from their own recollections. It can only add to the picture.

Make a habit of rounding (a term made popular by the healthcare industry, meaning "walk around and talk with your people") with team members individually before due dates. One-on-one conversations create a safer environment for asking questions. Once this is a habit, and therefore an expectation, debriefing can be a valued time for feedback for both parties.

If common themes emerge during debriefing, share these with the entire team. If you have a piece of information you *think* everyone would benefit from knowing, share that, too.

Clarity keeps the energy of productivity going. It's anticipatory of questions that can arise down the line. Make clarity a priority and your results (and your team) will benefit.

Rate yourself – and ask others to rate you – on this:

I consistently follow-up on the tasks and initiatives my team is working on.

(low)　　1　　2　　3　　4　　5　　(high)

Self-perception:

_____

_____

_____

Feedback from others:

_____

_____

_____

_____

_____

Reading 18

● ● ●

REMEMBER: ATTITUDE IS NOT EVERYTHING

I love this quote from *Batman Begins*:

"Bruce, deep down you may still be that same great kid you used to be. But it's not who you are underneath... it's what you do that defines you."

As a leader, parent, and trainer, I confess that I cringe when I hear someone try to pump people up with an "attitude is everything" approach.

While it sure is helpful to our own motivation to have a great attitude, it is unwise to focus on the "attitudes" of others, especially as a "cure-all".

Why?

Sometimes, a person can have a great attitude, but be a negative influence on others. If I enter a group with an excited, take charge, can-do attitude, I might be totally ignoring the personalities of the other members. What if the other members of my team like to take a slow, considered approach?

And what if that's the best way? My attitude might just mess things up, or at least show disrespect.

This can harm relationships and get in the way of achieving things. Then, what I learn is this: having a great attitude is a bad idea. Not totally true; using inconsiderate *behavior* is a bad idea. A subtle and critical difference.

Some days, a person can have a terrible attitude. If that person has learned that "attitude is everything," then on that day, that person might not try. If a team member thinks, "My attitude is terrible today, so I am useless," then their contribution will surely suffer, *and* their day will probably be lousy. That person is wrong about attitude: if their *behavior* contributes, then that is what matters, and can move the team forward, even on a bad day.

If you are the boss/manager/coach/teacher/leader, and you see a "bad attitude" on your team, it is generally useless to address the attitude, because it is nebulous and internal. However, if you focus on the *behavior*, you can experience success. Consider these two approaches:

[**weak**] "Hey Julie, shape up that attitude! You're bringing everybody down. Fire up!"

[**strong**] "Say Julie, when you act grumpy by frowning and sticking to one word answers to open-ended questions, that keeps us from being as productive as possible. Sorry you're having a rough day, really. We need your contributions, though, so can you soldier on and give us your thoughtful insights, please?"

Focus on ***behavior*** instead of attitude and see what happens.

Rate yourself – and ask others to rate you – on this:

I focus on the behavior of my team members. If efficiency or production is falling short, I address behaviors, rather than attitudes.

(low)   1   2   3   4   5   (high)

Self-perception:

_____

_____

_____

Feedback from others:

_____

_____

_____

_____

_____

Reading 19

●　●　●

ENCOURAGE INITIATIVE BY ASKING FOR IT

When I work with high level managers who direct other managers or team leaders, I frequently hear this frustration: "I want them to initiate more on their own – to do more of what needs to be done without being asked." Well, here are two truths:

1. You have to ask. In early stages, very specifically. In later stages, it can be as simple as "You are expected to initiate things and not wait to be asked. What is one thing you know you could do — and would do if asked — but aren't doing right now?" People aren't psychic. So, ask for what you want.
2. Do you want to be promoted, or considered a potential leader, or get other awards in the form of fellowships, titles, opportunities, or unique letters of recommendation?

Initiate things without being asked. Self-starters WIN, because they are rare. You are the person that everybody wants to hire, promote, honor, and/ or be around.

Be psychic, and do what your leader needs without being asked.

This is an attempt at a challenge, and I hope it doesn't come across as sarcastic, because it is meant to be helpful while challenging:

Leaders who complain about their followers being "lazy" because they don't initiate more might be perceived as "lazy" by observers, because they aren't doing the hard work of asking and guiding.

Rate yourself – and ask others to rate you – on this:

I actively guide my team in the right direction of what work needs to be done (without assuming they should just know). OR If I ever think "they should <u>know</u> that," I spell out what I'm thinking.

(low)   1   2   3   4   5   (high)

Self-perception:

_____

_____

_____

Feedback from others:

_____

_____

_____

_____

_____

Reading 20

AVOID SAYING "SHOULD"

There is enormous value in the principles in the book *Drive* by Dan Pink. If, as research has shown, people are motivated by autonomy, then there is a class of words we ought to avoid, as they can crush autonomy. These may include "ought," or "must," but let's focus on the one that seems to pass the most judgment:

"Should."

"Ought" is a little softer, and "must" is so strong that its intention is more obvious.

"Should," however, is more ominous, and implies something about the speaker's attitude toward the listener's ability to make their own decisions.

Can you feel it — the judgment? The moral superiority?

"You should roll it all into a 401(k)."

"You should post on Twitter more often."

"You should outsource your accounting."

"You should get the steak when you eat there."

You're thinking – What if I need more liquidity because I have health problems? What if I find frequent Tweeters annoying, and don't wanna be "that guy"? What if I enjoy numbers and want to know financials better than anyone else? What if that's none of your business? What if I love fish?

"Should" implies superior knowledge. "Should" implies superior judgment. And "should" can deny personhood.

Instead, say:

"An option I've explored is a 401(k) – want to hear more?"

"Twitter seems like a good avenue for your thoughts."

"If you outsource your accounting, you might sleep better at night." (Note: this is a behavior-outcome statement.)

"Their steak is amazing, if you're a beef-lover."

Using the behavior-outcome model:

If you avoid using the word "should," you'll give people more dignity.

or

When you say "should," here's what happens; you rob the listener of dignity (or autonomy, or personhood, or judgment).

You get the idea.

Rate yourself – and ask others to rate you – on this:

I am careful to eliminate the word "should" from any directives I give my team members.

(low)   1   2   3   4   5   (high)

Self-perception:

_____

_____

_____

Feedback from others:

_____

_____

_____

_____

_____

Reading 21

AVOID SAYING "DON'T"

Don't say don't.

Really. Two reasons for this: one is pretty esoteric and provokes skepticism, but the second is nearly self-evident:

1) Some research shows that the use of words/phrases involving "not" or "-n't" are subconsciously turned into the positive by the listener, because negative talk is rejected. So if a person is told "don't be late!" they actually perceive "be late," increasing the likelihood of non-compliance.

Some experts think that's reason enough to change what we say. I'm skeptical of that. However, this is a good reason:

2) Consistent negative talk will create a negative culture. A constant drumbeat of "don't forget" "don't be late" "don't screw that up" "don't talk to me right now" can be pretty discouraging. If you can rephrase things using positive words, a better atmosphere is created. Better atmosphere = more encouraging = more productive.

Lots of words can be used to address behavior you want to stop. Stop, avoid, limit, resist the temptation to, watch out for, etc. Throw in a courtesy word, and you've gone from ogre to uncle, without lowering your standards:

"Please stop using the copier during the meeting."

"Resist the temptation to have your phone out, please."

"Limit your talking to the topic, please."

"Always arrive on time, please."

"Please remember to fax the form by noon."

AND of course... **Please avoid use of the word "don't."**

Rate yourself – and ask others to rate you – on this:

I am careful to avoid using the word "don't" when directing my team members.

(low)   1   2   3   4   5   (high)

Self-perception:

_____

_____

_____

Feedback from others:

_____

_____

_____

_____

Reading 22

● ● ●

AVOID SHUTTING DOWN COMMUNICATION

Leaders avoid saying things that shut down discussion and communication.

The temptation is strong. Sometimes, when you're ready to move on, you may use one of the phrases below to be efficient. Or, you're not at your best and you're anxious to get out of the conversation.

Whatever your reason, the impact of these words will send the message that you want to shut the exchange down. Using them can be damaging to your credibility.

Here are some examples:

"...Enough said." or the colloquial "'nuf said."

"Last time I checked," followed by something like "this was still a free country."

"Just sayin'"

"No offense, but…"

"Yes, BUT..."

A great alternative to the last one is "yes, *and...*" or, "maybe... it's *also* true that..."

In your next give-and-take, especially if it's heated, ask yourself (or put on a sticky note in front of you):

"Is my language shutting down the conversation, or keeping it open?" And remember to sometimes just say, "I don't know – what do YOU think?"

Rate yourself – and ask others to rate you – on this:

I make a conscious effort to keep discussion and communication open, rather than using phrases that might shut it down.

(low)   1   2   3   4   5   (high)

Self-perception:

_____

_____

_____

Feedback from others:

_____

_____

_____

_____

_____

Reading 23

● ● ●

AVOID SAYING "INAPPROPRIATE"

One year, at the Iowa Employment Conference, I heard an employment law expert point out that the word "inappropriate" has no place in employee handbooks. He went on to say this is because courts have ruled time and again that the word "inappropriate" as a descriptor of behavior, dress, and language is too subjective and too vague to be enforceable.

Well, if that's true in case law, what might it mean for leaders who understand the value of specificity in feedback and other communication?

It means that "inappropriate" is being used as a substitute for something more specific, something better, and you can take that opportunity to make a more suitable (i.e. specific) substitution.

Leaders use "inappropriate" because it's safe; it doesn't force them into getting specific, and it might spare offending someone or making someone feel micromanaged.

Stop taking the easy way out, and use something more specific instead. Here are a few detailed examples to help you practice –

Avoid saying: "Those comments were so inappropriate. I don't want to hear anything like that again. Is that clear?"

Instead, say: "Telling Shawna that her idea 'sucks' isn't the way we communicate around here. Next time, please find better words, and definitely avoid 'sucks' in the future. Okay?"

Avoid saying: "Please don't meet clients in inappropriate places for presentations."

Instead, say: "When presenting to clients in off-site locations, consider coffee shops, quiet restaurants, and other places without loud behavior or excessive drinking around you. Nightclubs, sports bars (even Jethro's), and raves are off-limits for client presentation meetings. If you're unclear, please ask me. Thanks."

Avoid saying: "Stop with the inappropriate behavior at reception."

Instead, say: "Nail clipping, painting, and/or filing may be done in the locker room or outside the back door, and never in reception or in anyone's office."

Using the word "inappropriate" as a catch-all is too vague. Define what you really mean in order to connect with folks, get what you need, and increase engagement.

Rate yourself – and ask others to rate you – on this:

I avoid using the word "inappropriate" to describe someone's behavior because there is a better, more specific description for their actions.

(low)   1   2   3   4   5   (high)

Self-perception:

_____

_____

_____

Feedback from others:

_____

_____

_____

_____

Reading 24

●　●　●

NEVER BE SARCASTIC. EVER.

When I was in 6th grade, my music teacher, Mr. Jones, played us some *Switched-On Bach* – Bach performed on synthesizer.

That was pretty cool back in 1980. If you're over 40, I bet you know what I'm talking about. It actually got me really interested in "real" Bach music – I'm a fan to this day.

Mr. Jones was a real advocate, and fed me more to listen to, and encouraged my unusual (for a 6th-grade boy) passion for Baroque music. Until one day…

The big payoff at the end of the year (if we were good) was the "Rock and Roll Filmstrip Series." (Again, you gotta be over 40 to dig all these references. Sorry.)

When Mr. Jones announced this was coming, he said offhand, "Then there's Alan. All he wants to listen to is Bach!"

Classmates laughed, of course. Mr. Jones smiled at me, as if to say "Just kidding. I know you can handle it. I only 'pick on the people I really like.'"

I was embarrassed, sure, but more so, I felt betrayed. Who was this guy? Was he the one who encouraged my Bach passion, or the one who made fun of it? Jerk.

Fast forward to recent history, where I am the jerk:

After one witty exchange with an acquaintance, in which I was extremely funny (really, quite hilarious, I assure you), my wife said to me:

"You know, when you're sarcastic, it keeps people guessing. Even people who know you well. Do you really want that?"

No. Who am I? The one who encourages genuine connection and positive relationships (for a living!), or the one who uses them for cheap laughs? Jerk.

Effective leadership requires positive relationships, which require genuine connection, which isn't possible with sarcasm, or "only picking on the people you like."

There is no place for sarcasm in effective leadership. Humor, yes! Sarcasm – picking on people – no. Sorry. While it may be hilarious, it keeps people guessing, and wary.

And you don't want that.

Rate yourself – and ask others to rate you – on this:

In an effort to encourage genuine connection with my team, I avoid using sarcasm.

(low)   1   2   3   4   5   (high)

Self-perception:

_____

_____

_____

Feedback from others:

_____

_____

_____

_____

Reading 25

● ● ●

KNOW WHEN TO AVOID GIVING FEEDBACK

Feedback from leaders drives engagement and performance, yet workers report that feedback is lacking. Leaders even know this truth, but still avoid giving feedback.

Here are two reasons why it might be wise to delay giving feedback:

"I've been piling on – everything I tell this person has been critical lately; I feel badly about that."

This is an important realization – look in the mirror. If you've been focusing on the negative and avoiding the positive, then make an effort to find ways this person has contributed, and acknowledge them with positive feedback. Once you achieve balance again, give the corrective feedback.

Another possibility, though, is this; there is truly nothing to give positive feedback about. In that case, it's time to ditch the casual feedback and get formal. Have the serious crucial conversation, develop plans, and begin intensive coaching.

Is there a middle ground between those two options? Perhaps not. This is either a big, tough moment for you, or for them. Something needs to change.

"I'm in a bad mood, and I'm going to come across grumpy."

Good move. Give no critical feedback if you will end up seeming even slightly more "mad" than you actually are. The receiver of feedback exaggerates that emotion on their end, and will end up feeling far more "corrected" than you intend.

There are two ways to deal with this:

1. Wait until you are in a better state of mind.
2. Give a lot of appreciative or positive feedback to people around you. It will improve your mood. Research indicates that a 3 to 1 ratio of positive to critical feedback is effective for increasing engagement. This will be re-emphasized in upcoming readings.

Rate yourself – and ask others to rate you – on this:

I am careful not to give corrective feedback when I am in a "bad mood".

(low)   1   2   3   4   5   (high)

Self-perception:

_____

_____

_____

Feedback from others:

_____

_____

_____

_____

_____

Reading 26

● ● ●

LEARN FROM DISNEY'S CUSTOMER SERVICE MAGIC

Something that strikes most visitors to Walt Disney World is how "nice" of a place it is. It's very clean. The employees are called "cast members" because they're playing a role and they have a reputation for great service and friendliness. Everyone knows that.

But there's another unique element present at Disney World that is seemingly beyond the control of the Mouse. The guests at Disney World seem to be more well behaved, happier, and positive than guests at other places of business and entertainment. Most of us probably attribute this to the cleanliness and friendliness of Disney and its staff. But there is something else at play.

In #16 "Be Specific," we referred to the "behavior-outcome statement". The staff at Disney—the cast members—use behavior-outcome statements also. All the time.

A couple of examples:

"Please move all the way down, filling in all available space–front to back and left to right–to make room for everyone."

At a lot of places where people need to make room like this, instruction usually goes like this: "Squeeze in, people." Most people would probably sort of comply.

But, the Disney version offers the outcome (to make room for everyone) and that gives people a reason why. Further, the command itself begins the pleasantry, "please," and is also very specific. Specific behavior + polite words + reasonable outcome = willing cooperation.

Some attractions start with a pre-show. This creates the great illusion that your experience is started– even when it hasn't. In one case (Ellen's Energy Adventure), there's a short film shown in a large carpeted open space. On a hot day, before the film started, I sat down on the floor. Mara (my daughter) laid on the floor beside me with her head on my knee and Julie (my wife) laid down on the floor in the other direction with her head on my other knee. It was a lovely family moment, but it was soon shattered by the cast member's announcement:

"If you are lying or sitting on the floor, please stand up. We need to make room for anyone else who comes in, and anyone who comes in will be entering a dark room from the bright outside, so you know, they might step on you. So, please stand for the whole eight-minute pre-show."

In other places, a staff member would likely make an announcement like "Stand up everybody. No sitting or lying down in here." But the Disney way involved the specific behaviors, and the specific reason why, along with a bonus; we were told exactly how long we would be standing. Despite the pleasant comfort of our position, we cheerfully obeyed.

Next time you go to Disney World, watch for this. It is a great example of front-line employees, or organization members, exhibiting leadership behaviors.

If people at the lowest level of an organization (front-line employees) can motivate people outside of the organization (guests) with proactive communication that focuses on behavior, imagine how effective it can be if such an approach becomes the norm in your organization, and for you as a leader.

It can be magic.

Rate yourself – and ask others to rate you – on this:

I consistently make requests using specific language to describe behavior in the behavior-outcome model.

(low)   1   2   3   4   5   (high)

Self-perception:

_____

_____

_____

Feedback from others:

_____

_____

_____

_____

_____

Reading 27

● ● ●

KNOW HOW TO GIVE CRITICISM

Criticism is received fairly well when the relationship is strong between the parties. When you've built that bond with a team member, it's more likely that they detect your faith in their potential. Coach John Robinson said, "Never criticize until the person is convinced of your unconditional confidence in their abilities." In other words, Coach was never critical of a person unless he had faith in them, and they knew it.

When I think of the people in my life that I willingly take criticism and feedback from, without taking it personally (though my family and friends may point out that I still get a bit defensive), I realize the following:

They have faith in me. Think of the people who get defensive when you address or criticize them. Do they KNOW without a doubt that you have TOTAL faith in them? Or are they normal, and somewhat (or a lot) insecure?

Once you get to a great professional relationship, and they know you believe in them, you can start to give critical feedback. Until you hit that point, it will be less effective.

IMPORTANT: Continue to give positive feedback to reinforce that faith, at a ratio of 3 to 1, positive to corrective. Make it specific, and allow it to stand on its own. Combining criticism with positive feedback is unwise; the recipient might interpret this mixed message as your lack of faith that they can handle the criticism, or that your positive feedback is a manipulative attempt to "soften them up" for the "real" criticism.

Rate yourself – and ask others to rate you – on this:

I consistently give positive feedback in a ratio of three to one, positive to corrective.

(low)   1   2   3   4   5   (high)

Self-perception:

_____

_____

_____

Feedback from others:

_____

_____

_____

_____

Reading 28

● ● ●

IGNORE THE TONE

"**S**amantha, please reinstate the afternoon tea and coffee cart for the residents, starting in November."

Samantha [delivered with sarcastic tone and an eye roll]: "Well, sure, why not. Last time we tried it, Beth in 4C took 10 tea bags, and when I wasn't looking, some of the staff drained the second pot of coffee and I had to make a third one. [This is where the eye roll comes in] I can't wait to start it up again."

Because sarcasm has no place in effective workplace communication, you might be tempted to address the sarcasm. Or, the eye roll. Or, the clear pushback. While that would be acceptable, and likely desirable in the long term...

You have an opportunity here to send a message about ignoring sarcasm and having no time for silly pushback.

Do this instead. Totally ignore the tone of voice and focus on the message, being careful to avoid passive/aggressive tone yourself, and reply:

"Great. Thanks for taking care of that. I know you feel it's wasteful and a hassle; the day before we start it up again, let's spend a few minutes on some ideas to avoid that this next time around. Thanks for your time."

In that response, you've:

1. Ignored the tone, yet showed that you heard the concerns.
2. Kept things positive, even though Samantha wanted to inject drama.
3. Taken advantage of an opportunity to be an ally and a problem solver (needs-meeter).

It's good to address tone of voice and enforce high standards of respectful communication, and it makes sense to do so separately from the current issue, otherwise, the waters are muddied.

Stay alert for these opportunities.

Rate yourself – and ask others to rate you – on this:

When met with sarcasm or other blatant pushback, I ignore tone and focus on the message while acknowledging frustrations.

(low)   1   2   3   4   5   (high)

Self-perception:

_____

_____

_____

Feedback from others:

_____

_____

_____

_____

_____

Reading 29

● ● ●

MEET WITH YOUR PEOPLE, ONE-ON-ONE

Some think a weekly one-on-one is just for the corporate environment, between full-time, salaried workers and their supervisors.

One-on-ones truly work in a variety of environments, though.

I've had a client in a medical clinic who added monthly one-on-ones with all of their staff. Unorthodox in that environment, but it has resulted in lots of valuable employee-suggested improvements.

Weekly. Even for part-time employees? Yes. First rule of thumb – meet in private. It could be in your office, or at your cubicle desk. Use sensitivity and caution when other employees are close by.

The intention is to spend thirty minutes discussing three basic matters of business:

Ten minutes on the employee's questions and/or issues. Ten minutes on the manager/boss's questions and/or issues. Ten minutes on development by figuring out what's next.

With a little questioning and a sincere willingness to listen (as shown by eye contact and open posture) any questions or issues the employee has will likely come right out.

Once both parties' questions/issues are resolved, or have a plan for resolution, begin to discuss what's next. Are there other projects the employee could be doing? Would you like for her to research something else?

This is also the perfect opportunity to provide positive feedback. Strive for that ratio of 3:1, positive feedback to critical feedback.

One-on-ones are a valuable checkpoint. Used correctly, and frequently, they will help your team become more cohesive.

Rate yourself – and ask others to rate you – on this:

To keep work and communication flowing freely, I meet with my team members one-on-one on a regular basis.

(low)   1   2   3   4   5   (high)

Self-perception:

_____

_____

_____

Feedback from others:

_____

_____

_____

_____

_____

Reading 30

● ● ●

SAY IT ALL

A true staff meeting story:

Tyler turned to Tykeshia and said, "I never know where I stand with you."

Tykeshia replied, "Don't worry. When you screw something up, I'll tell you. You're doing just fine."

Tyler looked back to Tykeshia and summoned his courage, and said, "I'm sorry. That just doesn't work for me. I need to know if I'm on track or not."

Something that leaders sometimes think is, "I don't need to tell people when they're doing things right. That's just their job. It's almost insulting to give compliments about the normal stuff they do."

There may be some truth to that, but this is also true: People need to know how they're doing. It engages and motivates them.

This is also very true: research shows that people thrive more when they receive three bits of positive feedback for every one bit of corrective feedback.

(On balance. Please avoid taking this to mean that you ought to package things in bundles of four.)

If you've studied best practices in leadership, then you know there are times you must provide corrective feedback to others.

If both of these things are true, then this makes sense:

Give people positive feedback when they're on the right track – even if it's just affirmation that they are doing their jobs correctly. They'll stay more engaged, because they'll know they're on track, and be more receptive to critical feedback when it occurs.

Both of these improve engagement, and improve relationships. Once Tykeshia started telling Tyler both the correct things he was doing, the things he needed to improve upon, both Tyler's engagement and their relationship improved. Tykeshia enjoyed working with Tyler more, because open communication builds strong work relationships, and keeps people from guessing and stressing.

So go ahead and tell people when they're doing things right. Bonus: it also shows you don't take them for granted.

Rate yourself – and ask others to rate you – on this:

I regularly affirm my team members when they're doing what's expected.

(low)   1   2   3   4   5   (high)

Self-perception:

_____

_____

_____

Feedback from others:

_____

_____

_____

_____

SECTION FIVE: MODELING

Modeling

It's cliché to mock the "do as I say, not as I do" leadership failure. That's because this failure is way too common.

Leaders must consistently model the behavior they expect from others.

Modeling flows directly from integrity. Integrity is the leader's *commitment* to consistency. Modeling is the tangible *display* of that commitment through behavior. Let's revisit examples from reading 11, with that in mind:

If you expect your front-line folks to provide great customer service, then use the same standards of interaction when you talk to those folks.

If you expect the people who report to you to return communications promptly, then respond to their communications promptly.

If you expect your meeting participants to keep their technology set aside during meetings, then you'd best never get yours out, either.

"People look at you and me to see what they are supposed to be. And, if we don't disappoint them, maybe, just maybe, they won't disappoint us."
– Walt Disney

Reading 31

● ● ●

MODEL THE BEHAVIOR YOU EXPECT

Once, I planned an event that took place at a hotel, and I needed to check in eight rooms at once. The front desk was busy, and so I understood that I needed to wait my turn. No problem. However, the two employees checking people in were *not* moving very quickly. It was as though they felt no sense of urgency at all, and with a full lobby. It's not that they were thorough, they were... *slow*. And kind of cold. This made me a touch impatient. Then, the manager (well-dressed, cheerful, smiling) arrived on the scene, and I was momentarily relieved.

Momentarily.

Because here's what I pictured:

The manager would swoop in, station himself at the middle, unused computer, smile and say "Who's next?" And, because I was next, I would step up, tell him about the eight rooms I needed to check in, and he would smile, and say something like "I can take care of that for you," and proceed to very *obviously*, and very quickly, and very efficiently **show those other two employees how it's done around here.** With a smile!

Here's what *actually* happened:

Manager: "Have you been helped?"

Me: "No, not yet, but that's okay – it's busy, huh? Lots of birthday parties, it looks like."

Manager: "Yeah, it's crazy."

Me: "I just need to check in eight rooms."

Manager: "EIGHT!?"

Me: "Yup, I've got a couple groups here."

Manager: [gesturing to the employee to his right] "Then *she* can help you." [laughs, turns away, and leaves.]

Seriously.

So, I waited longer. No problem. They were busy. Plus, they were doing things exactly as they had learned around here. What more could I expect?

The next morning, a needed training room was locked. I went to the front desk to let them know that it was locked. Simple oversight, and simple to fix, right? It just needed to be unlocked by 8:00 a.m.

It was unlocked at 8:20.

It was a nice place, with nice people. What would it be like if the managers modeled the behavior that ought to be expected?

Ever seen a train? Ever seen the cars pass the engine? Never. If you're a leader, and you do things at level 10, your followers will likely do them at an "8".

If you have a rough day, and your effort is a "7", expect your followers to be at a "5".

Leaders model the way by setting the example for others in ways that are consistent with their values. This promotes consistent progress and building of commitment.

Let's get to work!

Rate yourself – and ask others to rate you – on this:

I consistently lead by example, actively demonstrating the behaviors I request from my team.

(low)   1   2   3   4   5   (high)

Self-perception:

_____

_____

_____

Feedback from others:

_____

_____

_____

_____

Reading 32

KNOW YOU'RE BEING CONSTANTLY OBSERVED

I once ordered a coffee from someone who made no eye contact with me, and waited for me to initiate the order with no greeting.

I had watched this go down with the three people ahead of me in line, also. They stepped up, placed their orders with the cashier, who looked down with her finger poised above the buttons. As the order was placed, she kept looking down, and spoke only these words: "Is that it?" and "$3.56" (or whatever the total was).

The other thing I witnessed was this: she had a small problem and had a question for her supervisor. She looked at the feet of the supervisor, sideways, when she asked for help.

The supervisor gave a curt, nearly rude answer, while looking the other way doing nothing in particular.

Aha!

On the way out, I saw a "now hiring" placard that said "looking for workers to make a day-brightening experience for our customers!!!"

At some point, this woman had surely been told to provide better, more proactive service, but she didn't see that from her leader. People don't do what we ask them to do. People do what they see their leaders do.

Rate yourself – and ask others to rate you – on this:

I remain aware that my team __and__ customers may be observing me even during routine moments, and I stay consistent even then.

(low)   1   2   3   4   5   (high)

Self-perception:

_____

_____

_____

Feedback from others:

_____

_____

_____

_____

_____

Reading 33

DELIVER TO THOSE YOU LEAD

Remember that two-word definition of leadership – "Meet Needs"?

You can really put that into action by staying conscious of things that you can deliver to the people who report to you.

Your team is so used to deliverables *they're* accountable for, that it's a nice change of pace when you ask them specifically,

"What can *I* deliver to *YOU*?"

Perhaps you've asked for a set of account reviews to be completed. You could ask, "Would you like me to tell you which of these are the five most important to me?"

Maybe you've put someone in charge of inventory. You could say, "I have a free hour next Tuesday – how could I use that hour to help you move this project forward?"

You may have delegated one of your usual tasks to a high-potential team member. You could offer, "Now that you're underway, is there one aspect you'd like to delegate back to me to see how I'd handle it, or just because you've gotten unexpectedly busy and you'd appreciate the help?"

Consider asking your team occasionally, "What can I deliver to YOU?"

Rate yourself – and ask others to rate you – on this:

I seek to meet needs by occasionally asking my team members what they need from me to help with their work.

(low)   1   2   3   4   5   (high)

Self-perception:

_____

_____

_____

Feedback from others:

_____

_____

_____

_____

Reading 34

● ● ●

SHARE, ABUNDANTLY

There is a lot of value in picking up the phone to ask for help, information, or other assistance from fellow professionals. But, on the flip side, what do you do when you're the one who receives that call?

Share. Abundantly.

In my former profession, many of us Iowa band directors worked toward the special singular honor of representing our class at the annual Bandmasters Convention. This was a big honor that went to just one (or zero) programs per year.

One year, a colleague (David) and I set a goal: One of our programs would make it.

For weeks on end, while preparing the audition, we recorded our groups and emailed the recordings to each other. We would listen, critique, and head back to work. Understand that this was a very competitive process, but we set that aside for the goal of improving our teaching and our students' experience.

At the end of the process, one of our groups was selected. The next year, the other group made it. The abundant, open sharing made it possible.

In the training and consulting profession, intellectual property can be closely guarded. So can personal information about running the business end of things.

Some of my material comes from a man named Tim. As I realized I was about to use a bit of his content and some of his activities for financial gain, I went to him to tell him this and ask how he felt. "Will you use it to build people?" he asked. "Well, yeah, but I'll make money, too."

"I don't care about the money. I care about the people. If you're building, steal away." What a great model! When someone came to me a couple of years later to ask "Can I use some of your stuff?" I had no choice but to give the same answer.

Have you ever experienced an Open Space Symposium? It's a conference where experts share freely of knowledge with no compensation – and no holding back. It's "risky" in the eyes of some, but everyone benefits.

When I was getting started in this business, it was tough to learn details, like "how does a proposal look?" and "how much should I charge?" You can find websites on this stuff, but they're not reliable enough. There are books, but they aren't specific enough. There were two people who shared any and all information with me. After a conversation with one man, he said "Alan, you now know more about my finances than anybody but my accountant."

So, guess what I do when I get asked similar questions? No choice, but to share abundantly. So glad I had the right role models on this, or I might have chosen the (sadly) more common path of guardedness. So, thanks to David, and Tim, and others who have set the stage for this way of doing business.

Because I've noticed that those who share, and give, and stay open, tend to be happier and more secure. Whew.

Rate yourself – and ask others to rate you – on this:

When asked for help by my peers, I openly and abundantly share whatever I can.

(low)   1   2   3   4   5   (high)

Self-perception:

_____

_____

_____

Feedback from others:

_____

_____

_____

_____

_____

Reading 35

● ● ●

MASTER NEW SKILLS

To know, and not do, is to not yet know. - Karl Lewin

Have you ever explained how to tie your shoes? Better yet, was there ever a time that you tried tying shoes simply based on a verbal description of the process? You had to DO it to get it, right? That's what Lewin is getting at.

Have you ever read a great article or book with a new leadership idea that you couldn't wait to implement? Sure hope so! Ever given up because it was clumsy - or because the process intimidated you? You're not alone.

It is true that we ought to try new things. It is also true that when we do, we might be lousy at them. Lots of people give up at that point. The successful don't. They push through the clumsy attempts at new good ideas — and end up setting themselves apart from the crowd, just because they stuck to the new way of giving feedback, or running a meeting, or employing a task management system.

Flip it around — do the people you lead nail everything the first time? Hopefully not, otherwise their jobs are too easy. Do you make it safe to make mistakes, AND maintain the high standards that they must reach after they push through the mistakes? That's the sloppy, clumsy part of nailing new skills.

It's sloppy, though, to not coach others – and ourselves– after a mistake, failure, or clumsy attempt.

Here are some debrief questions:

- How can this lesson apply to your next project?
- What will you do differently next time?
- What could someone else on the team do to help you next time?

Feel free to explore other questions, but make sure they're focused on the future and the next opportunity.

It's useless to know, unless you do. Push through, and make it safe and expected for others to DO as well.

Rate yourself – and ask others to rate you – on this:

I make it safe for myself and my team members to make mistakes along the way.

(low)   1   2   3   4   5   (high)

Self-perception:

_____

_____

_____

Feedback from others:

_____

_____

_____

_____

SECTION SIX: STRETCHING AND GROWING

—Stretching and Growing—

L eaders are committed to constant self-improvement.

Why use the phrase "stretching and growing?" Growing isn't descriptive enough. Anything that grows has to change; nothing just "gets bigger." There are changes, and some of them can be uncomfortable, even painful.

In order to grow, we have to "stretch." "Stretching" implies action, reaching, pushing, and willingly entering into discomfort and attempts to change. So, leaders have to stretch in order to grow.

One of two things is *always* true:

1. I am a perfect master of all my desired skills and capabilities; I'm perfect. Or,
2. I still have room to grow.

If you fall in category number 2, then what are you going to do about it? What are you going to do differently tomorrow than today? What specific personal growth efforts do you consistently undertake? Who do you stay accountable to?

The best leaders have ready answers to those questions. "You can't think yourself into a new way of acting; you must act yourself into a new way of thinking." — Clifford Madsen

Rate yourself – and ask others to rate you – on this:

I acknowledge that I always have room to grow, and consistently work to add new skills and abilities to my repertoire.

(low)   1   2   3   4   5   (high)

Self-perception:

_____

_____

_____

Feedback from others:

_____

_____

_____

_____

Reading 36

●　●　●

STAND OUT

In preparation for a breakout session at a conference, I developed a list of things a leader can do to stand out and get noticed. Not in a "look at me!" kind of way, but in a way that will help the leader connect more to others, and to enable others to connect as well.

Some of this guidance appeared in earlier readings, but they are presented here, together, as we start to explore active stretching and growing.

While all ten pointers are applicable to all potential leaders, there are four that newer, more fast-paced leaders, might relate to more than the experienced. Let's take a look at those first:

1) Never have the last word.

Strong leaders are tempted to consider many discussions to be arguments or debates – opportunities to change hearts and minds. Carnegie says it well – you can never win an argument. If you lose, you lose. If you win, you lost. Letting others have the last word will empower them and *set you apart* as thoughtful.

2) Avoid using earbuds/headphones in public.

Not because it's rude, or associated with a younger generation, or because it may appear to be a selfish attempt to control your own environment; but because it interferes with your ability to connect. *Set yourself apart* by always being open to connection.

3) Use skillful writing mechanics.

The proliferation of fast electronic communication has made it acceptable to abbreviate words and truncate sentences. FWIW -> I do it 2. Sometimes. This is good news – it makes it easy to *set yourself apart* by using traditional methods like complete words and sentences. I heard an anecdote once about a college professor getting an email from a student who had to get out of a commitment. It was two paragraphs, well written. Think that student set herself apart? Absolutely.

4) Habitually use pleasantries and good etiquette.

Another casualty of speed and shortened communication is the use of "please", "thank you", and "you're welcome". Great news! If you make those words, and other polite conventions, your habit, it's easy to *set yourself apart*. "You're welcome" is the huge one; it conveys so much more openness and connecting than things like "yup" or "no prob," and honors the "thanker" more than "no, thank YOU."

The next few pointers apply to the experienced leader as well.

5) Whenever possible, communicate by phone or in person.

Is the person you need to visit with in the same building? Walk up the hall. Consider the number of emails and texts you deal with on a daily basis. Yes, they're convenient, but it's hard for any of them to stand out.

What if you are the person who makes conversation the default? You'll *stand out*. Warning — you might be annoying, too, if the person you're working to connect with much prefers the written word. Use with good judgment.

6) Stand in such a way as to be trusted and accepted.

Without going all-out on body language, just consider these two ideas: stand with your arms at your side (not in pockets, not crossed in front or back, not fidgety). Might feel weird at first, but research confirms this posture conveys the most openness and trustworthiness. Also, face the person speaking. Fully. Imagine a line from your nose to theirs – and keep it perpendicular to your shoulders. *Set yourself apart* by being the best-connecting listener.

7) Never interrupt.

Ever. Most people interrupt, and it's normal. *Set yourself apart* by never doing it. Makes people feel valued.

8) Take every opportunity to write hand-written notes.

Especially to say thank you. It's a lost art, and doesn't take much time. However, it conveys that you've taken time and care, and this impression will help you *stand out*.

9) Never be sarcastic.

It makes people wonder how you really feel. This uncertainty interferes with connection. *Stand out* by being sincere.

There are lots of ways to set yourself apart, to be sure. But these nine have the most payoff, based on how easily you can implement them.

If you set yourself apart, you will connect better, and with more people. Then, you stand a greater chance of doing some good in the world.

And remember, these tools are always to be used for good and not for evil. In every interaction, you have the power to make the world a better place. Why not do it?

Rate yourself – and ask others to rate you – on this:

I can cite examples in three of these areas where I set myself apart.

(low)   1   2   3   4   5   (high)

Self-perception:

_____

_____

_____

Feedback from others:

_____

_____

_____

_____

Reading 37

SOLVE INTERNAL FEUDS

When I was a young teacher, I often found myself in the middle of student disputes. My response was always something along the lines of "You need to learn how to solve your own problems." I was thinking I was doing them a service by empowering them to grow up and solve problems on their own. In reality, I was avoiding drama myself, and being selfish. Leaders of organizations need to clean up spats between people.

It is a cop-out to say "People need to solve their own personality issues," or "That's just the way he is; nothing I can do to change him."

These responses undermine the power of leadership. Also, you've missed an opportunity to improve the way your team works together.

If you have people in your organization who are too immature to solve their drama, then you have an opportunity to develop your people by teaching them how.

You also have a chance to demonstrate that you care, and that you're interested in seeing their lives become better. This isn't soft and flowery; this is practical stuff that will improve the effectiveness of your team, ensuring that more work gets done.

Effective leaders will become well versed on personality styles and how to identify them. That's not enough, though. It's also necessary to know the steps needed to teach people to communicate and work in ways that connect with all other styles.

Because that's what it usually is – a misfire of communication that leads to misunderstandings, that people inevitably chalk up to "personality conflicts," or immaturity.

Regardless of what you call it, the effective leader will step in to solve internal feuds.

Rate yourself – and ask others to rate you – on this:

Instead of using the old "solve it between yourselves" strategy, I take the opportunity to lead by solving internal feuds.

(low)   1   2   3   4   5   (high)

Self-perception:

_____

_____

_____

Feedback from others:

_____

_____

_____

_____

_____

Reading 38

● ● ●

MAKE CLUMSY ATTEMPTS TO DO THE RIGHT THING

Clumsy attempts at self-improvement are better than smooth successes at nailing the status quo. A good, and immediate, example is feedback.

I've never met anyone who launched a serious, sincere argument against that truism.

And yet, most leaders don't do it. Time gets in the way. Another obstacle: The belief that people should never be praised for doing "what they're supposed to be doing anyway." (The illusion is that feedback is praise. It's not.)

The most frequent obstacle, it seems? Discomfort.

You know from previous readings that leaders provide frequent, specific, behavior-based feedback that is more often positive than negative.

So if I know it helps to say things like, "Bill, you always do a great job stapling the cover pages to the TPS reports. Thanks, keep it up," then why don't I?

Because it's not a habit.

If I know it is actually non-threatening and relationship-building to say things casually like "Say, Bill, it really helps the folks in accounting keep things straight when you staple the cover pages to the TPS reports – will you please make sure to do it each time?" then why don't I?

Because it's not a habit.

Make it a habit, right? Easier said than done. Because the first time, it might come out like

"Bill – um, hey – Bill. Yeah, I was meaning to say, ah, that those people up in accounting really like the cover pages stapled to the reports – the TPS reports. And you do it like, all the time. And it's super helpful, even though it seems like a little thing. So um, keep doin' it, okay?"

And it feels clumsy, and may make you uncomfortable. Too bad. Leaders need to push their comfort zones to do uncomfortable things.

And Bill appreciates it. Because what would you normally say? Nothing. And Bill doesn't know how he's doing. Because you never tell him. Because it's not a habit yet.

An amazing thing is this: At one point in time, Michael Jordan was a lousy ball player. At first, Miles Davis had lousy trumpet-playing skills. At one point, you couldn't read. Clumsy attempts are needed before good things – then great things – happen. Make them. That's what leaders do.

Rate yourself – and ask others to rate you – on this:

Although it may feel clumsy and awkward, I make a consistent effort to make giving positive, specific feedback a habit.

(low)   1   2   3   4   5   (high)

Self-perception:

_____

_____

_____

Feedback from others:

_____

_____

_____

_____

_____

Reading 39

● ● ●

BE TRANSPARENT (WITHOUT TMI)

Transparency builds trust. Too many leaders have a habit of holding back information, which can look like information-hoarding, or secret-keeping. Those behaviors hurt trust.

But, leaders also know when to stop; leaders will avoid the temptation to share TOO much information. Leaders share information, as appropriate, to: A) keep people informed, B) keep people from wondering, and C) project confidence and security.

Examples of information-hoarding:

"Everything is fine and will continue as always around here. Don't let the rumors get to you."

"We're not sure why the plane isn't going to take off as scheduled. We're just going to sit tight on the tarmac here."

Examples of transparency:

"The rumors are painting a worst-case scenario. The reality is, we're in discussions right now on how to trim $300,000 from the budget enterprise-wide.

We will know more next week Friday, and I'll share that information with you as soon as I have it."

"There's a disabled plane on the runway; we're not sure how long it will take to clear it, but we have to sit tight until they do. I wish I could tell you how long it will take, but we just don't know. Sometimes it takes 10 minutes, sometimes an hour; once we know how bad it is, we'll let you know."

Examples of over-sharing:

"You think you're scared? I've been tasked to eliminate $120,000 by trimming some discretionary, and by eliminating a position. No matter what happens, it will hurt the department, and it will hurt me. I've been losing sleep over this for weeks, believe me."

"Yup, we're stuck on the tarmac. Disabled plane. If we're here for more than an hour, then we'll have to take you back to the gate and many of you will miss your connections. With the weather in Chicago, some of you could be stuck for days. Catering also shorted us on bottled water. And, this crew needs to be in Palm Beach by 9:00. You think you've got it bad now? Could get worse, way worse, and we are in a pretty foul mood up here in the cockpit, too, believe you me. Oh, wait, they've cleared it and we're third in line. Nevermind. We'll be in the air in 15 minutes. Enjoy your flight."

Where's the line? Finding it is certainly an art. Here's one measuring stick to help guide you:

Leaders might share too much information when they are insecure, "trying too hard," or are too stressed and looking for sympathy.

Rate yourself – and ask others to rate you – on this:

I make certain not to under or over-share information, particularly when stressed or insecure.

(low) 1 2 3 4 5 (high)

Self-perception:

_____

_____

_____

Feedback from others:

_____

_____

_____

_____

Reading 40

● ● ●

KNOW THAT ALL SOLUTIONS ARE A TEMPORARY RESTING PLACE

Jill was a jerk of a boss.

Her people didn't like her, mostly because she was bossy, passive-aggressive, and a bad communicator.

This all added up to a low-trust, high-tension situation.

Jill got good advice: Be nice. Build relationships. Build trust. Avoid bossiness.

It worked. For a while. Until the work started to fall behind. People took advantage of "nice Jill" after they realized she really had changed. Jill was frustrated again, for a new reason.

"Am I too nice, now?" She asked for more advice. And she got good advice: Be the boss. Without being bossy, be the boss; set goals, maintain high production standards, communicate them clearly and hold people accountable.

And it got better. Way better. Jill finally realized that all solutions are a temporary resting place.

We never really have it "all figured out." Sometimes, things go well, and we get lulled into complacency, thinking that now we've stumbled across "the formula."

But people evolve, situations change, and the circumstances of the changing world dictate that we stay nimble, self-aware, and ready to adopt a new point of view.

The "bumper sticker" to put in your line of sight when you find yourself in this state is this:

"All solutions are a temporary resting place." – Ronald Heifetz

Rate yourself – and ask others to rate you – on this:

I remain self-aware, ready to adapt when new solutions need to be formed.

(low)   1   2   3   4   5   (high)

Self-perception:

_____

_____

_____

Feedback from others:

_____

_____

_____

_____

_____

SECTION SEVEN: POSITIVITY

Positive Passion!

We've covered six leadership traits and skills. Now, it's time to talk about two mindsets that must permeate our leadership behaviors.

The first is positivity. Being positive is the way others see that the hard work is worth it.

Now, a leader ought not be a fake, smile-plastered, Pollyanna; positive leadership is not "soft" leadership. It *does* mean that leaders generally use positive language, display appropriate optimism (tempered with realism), and treat people kindly.

It is also falling short to simply preach a "positive attitude." While it *is* possible to control our attitude, and a positive attitude *does* make our day better and work easier, those around us do *not* see our attitude; they see our behavior.

So – have that positive attitude. Good plan. If it's a bad attitude day, though, you are not defeated. Stay positive in your words and body language around your folks, so they understand that the hard work is worth it.

> **"When enthusiasm is inspired by reason, is practical in application, reflects confidence, and spreads good cheer, raises morale, inspires associates, arouses loyalty, and laughs at adversity, it is beyond price." – Coleman Cox**

Rate yourself – and ask others to rate you – on this:

If you ask the people I interact with, they will tell you that I am optimistic.

(low)   1   2   3   4   5   (high)

Self-perception:

_____

_____

_____

Feedback from others:

_____

_____

_____

_____

Reading 41

● ● ●

KNOW POSITIVE LEADERSHIP ISN'T "SOFT" LEADERSHIP

Sometimes, when people are urged to take a positive approach to leadership, there is some pushback. Some people seem to equate "positivity" with being super-nice, but being kind is much deeper than a spewing of empty compliments like "good job" or "nice work" or "super!"

You can't be too kind. But, you *can* be too soft. That is the difference, and I'll admit that I have had trouble sometimes helping folks understand the difference. I just read *Good to Great* and have taken quite a liking to Jim Collins's phrase "rigorous, not ruthless." This is the message for leaders who would like to be positive.

Remember the "behavior-outcome statement" model from reading 16? This focus on behavior, and the high standards of the organization, can be done in a way that is positive, not negative. In a way that is rigorous, not ruthless.

There is a danger in being nice while enforcing high standards. If one continually says things like "please be quiet" or "I am just assuming that all this off task behavior has a purpose" with a smile, one can come off as appearing very passive-aggressive, which is on the edge of sarcasm, and sarcasm has no place in leadership; it is cheap and disrespectful. However, one does not need to be visibly angry or overly stern either. Team members who "buy in" will be more productive *and* more loyal.

One other way to enforce high standards and be kind is to remain very specific about behaviors. Saying to the whole staff "we all need to make sure we stay until the end of the shift", when there's just one or two people sneaking out early, does not help the cause. That is soft *and* negative at the same time. Taking aside an employee who skips out early and saying "you nearly always do good work; you do the most good when you stay till the end of your shift. Around here, we all work our shifts, unless there's something else going on that I don't know about. Is there anything wrong I need to know about? If not, you need to stay until the end of the shift." This sort of correction validates the employee's contribution and enforces the high standards. If your tone of voice is matter of fact, then you will *not* be stern, or mean. Because we have experienced so much stern or grumpy correction during our lives, a matter-of-fact correction or criticism will, over time, become part of a positive approach. An approach that upholds high standards *and* is very specific about behavior is positive, *but not soft*. Be rigorous, not ruthless.

Rate yourself – and ask others to rate you – on this:

I uphold high standards and maintain a positive environment by being specific about desired/undesired behavior.

(low)   1   2   3   4   5   (high)

Self-perception:

_____

_____

_____

Feedback from others:

_____

_____

_____

_____

Reading 42

● ● ●

BEWARE ACTING WHILE STRESSED

Decades ago, Walter Wangerin wrote a brilliant story about the way our approach can make a big difference in the lives of others – it was the main influencer of my credo "Everything you do makes a person's day better or worse. What are you going to do with that power?"

The format of that story — same setting, two different kinds of experiences — has been replicated in my life. Almost eerie, but cool. So – my real-life version follows.

Once, I got a car wash in Des Moines. The car was fairly new and the paint was intact at that time — no dings or scratches yet. When I examined it a bit later, though, I found a scratch. A very small hairline scratch, perhaps two inches long, just above the rear driver's side door. Barely noticeable, but real, and clearly caused by dirt or sand being in the brushes of the car wash. I required justice.

I was having a busy and stressful day, and this really put me over the edge. I complained. I was given a form to fill out to request compensation. It seemed to not see any action, so I returned, days later, and met with the owner. The owner and employee were slow to respond, and I got a little passive/aggressive in the interactions, and a couple weeks later, they finally relented to my pressure and complaints, and set up an appointment for me at a body shop for paint retouching for the scratch. Justice!

I'll bet I spent four hours on the issue, and put an extra 20 or so miles on my car, but I got Justice! And I felt terrible. It had taken a long time, I had to be a bit of a jerk, and it really wasn't that big of a deal in the grand scheme of things. My stress (and, frankly, feelings of powerlessness) had gotten the best of me.

Recently, while getting gas at a service station, I bought the add-on car wash at the pump. Just $8. When I pulled around to the car wash, though, it was being cleaned and was out of operation for the next couple hours. When I went to the register inside to get my money back, I was told that the car wash was a separate business, and that I'd have to call the owner. I did, and left a message about the situation. He didn't call me back for four days, and apologized for how long it took him to get back to me. I said this:

"No problem. Hey, if I was obsessing over this thing, I'd probably have some pretty messed-up priorities." He was really thankful for that attitude, and said that he wished everyone were so easy to deal with. He made the situation right. Justice! But this time, I felt better. Because I had treated the "offenders" better.

I wouldn't mind bumping into the last guy sometimes. But the previous car-wash people? I'd hide my face and hope they didn't remember me.

80% of decisions are made based on emotion, not reason. Also, we tend to act less mature when stressed. The lessons? There are many.

One is this; when stressed, see if you can delay acting, or speaking, or addressing a situation until the stress passes. This will increase the likelihood of a better decision, and (more importantly) better interactions and relationships. Be nice.

Rate yourself – and ask others to rate you – on this:

I respect the interactions I have with people by holding off acting when stressed until a time when I can communicate with even temperament.

(low)   1   2   3   4   5   (high)

Self-perception:

_____

_____

_____

Feedback from others:

_____

_____

_____

_____

Reading 43

● ● ●

USE THE PHRASE "AROUND HERE…"

My first boss was fond of saying, "Most days, we have fun **around here**." The first time I heard him say this was in my job interview. He followed it up with, "…and you can't say that about most jobs."

It was my first job, so I took his word for it. He was right, but I think part of the reason he was right was the consistency and relentlessness of his message, and the subtle lifting up of our situation. By using the words "around here," he was painting a picture of the organization's atmosphere/culture/vibe all the time, and it was also a way of controlling the organization's atmosphere/culture/vibe.

Smart. And like all smart ideas, worthy of using in other situations.

Back when I was a teacher, I started saying variations of, "The most important thing we do **around here** is treat each other with kindness and respect." I said it a lot, put it on written communication from time to time, and eventually it stuck. The students repeated it on cue.

It caught on, I think, for two reasons:

1. It was basically true most of the time, for most people.
2. It was a worthy goal that spoke to the needs of the people in the group.

It wasn't just a slogan, or a cute bit of indoctrination. It had a positive impact on our culture, and became a touchstone for enforcing community standards. This can work for you, too.

For example, if Tina lets her rough day get the best of her and she snaps at Laura, you could say, "Hey, Tina – I'm sorry you're having a bad day, but that's not how we treat each other **around here**, no matter what. Is there anything I can do to help you?"

When you add that last part, mean it sincerely. If Tina says, "I need time away from everybody," give it to her. (This is assuming that this was an isolated behavior. Repeated infractions of "what we do around here" call for a different course of action.)

Even things as simple as punctuality or accountability can be put into the culture.

"Say, Dylan, **around here**, we show up on time. Any reason you're late that I need to know about? Are you okay?" Asking those last two questions indicates that you have faith in Dylan, assuming the best of him, and that you regard his behavior as the exception, not the rule.

Assume the best about people, and you will generally receive it.

Rate yourself – and ask others to rate you – on this:

I actively participate in creating/maintaining our group culture by using the phrase "around here, we..."

(low)   1   2   3   4   5   (high)

Self-perception:

_____

_____

_____

Feedback from others:

_____

_____

_____

_____

_____

Reading 44

● ● ●

KEEP PEOPLE ON THE RIGHT TRACK

So far in the book, we've found several ways to communicate specific feed-back, both positive and critical. Now, let's be even more clear about the purpose; and if you've become a believer, consider communicating all of this to your team.

At a team meeting, declare your intention to be more purposeful with feed-back, both positive and critical. You might use words like these:

> "I am making a commitment to greater intentionality with feedback. I'm going to work to be specific with you all, to be unafraid to be critical, and to do a better job of letting you know you're on the right track by giving you ample affirming feedback. I'm aiming for a ratio of three bits of positive feedback for each bit of corrective feedback, and I'm not going to deliver all of them at once, but let each bit stand on its own."

If people are mostly doing what they're supposed to be doing, but only hear criticism, they will have the mistaken belief that they are doing a poor job. In an environment like this, morale, performance, and relationships suffer.

If people need critical feedback or performance coaching sometimes, but only hear positive feedback, they will have the mistaken belief that they're performing perfectly. That is until something causes a serious consequence and takes them by surprise.

The wariness this environment causes will also hurt morale, performance, and relationships.

Most people do well most of the time. And, most people prefer to work in a positive atmosphere.

The simplest way to keep people on the right track is to remember…

> THREE to ONE: give three bits of specific, affirming feedback for each bit of critical feedback.

Too much negative will hurt, but so will holding negative back.

This ratio will keep the atmosphere positive, and give team members a realistic view on how they're doing.

It will strengthen their understanding of what to keep doing, and what to change.

Research supports this as the way to keep engagement high.

Three to one. Give it a shot, be specific, and stay accountable to your team.

Rate yourself – and ask others to rate you – on this:

I have told my team of my intention to use a 3:1 ratio of positive to corrective feedback to maintain a positive, but effective, work environment.

(low)   1   2   3   4   5   (high)

Self-perception:

_____

_____

_____

Feedback from others:

_____

_____

_____

_____

_____

Reading 45

● ● ●

REMEMBER THE WORK

Have you seen productivity dip while creating a positive atmosphere? There's a likely reason, and a solution.

So much of this book's content is devoted to positive, encouraging, servant leadership. Every once in awhile, a leader comes along who is so committed to positivity that they wonder why productivity might be down, not up. They're usually missing something...

The **work**.

The work *has* to get done. The whole point of positive, encouraging servant leadership (in the context of WORK) is more about creating an environment of engagement to *set the stage* and *right the relationships* to ensure that work gets done.

Did you see that episode of *The Office* in which Michael starts his own paper company, and makes a workspace with Nerf balls and other goofy stuff? He's emulating that stereotype of the Silicon Valley workplaces loaded with ping-pong tables and beanbag chairs in order to promote creativity and innovation. He's missing a big thing – and so can we – the work.

If you want to emulate those happy happy things, you've also got to emulate the 80-hour weeks those people put in. The passion for creation that makes everything else slip away. The Michael Scott Paper Company forgot that part.

Your examples are likely not as extreme; if you do encounter a slowdown, and "blame" it on a greater commitment to positivity, double-check yourself on these questions:

Is at least 25% of your friendly, specific feedback *corrective*, rather than *complimentary*? When someone consistently falls short of expectations, do you have a *habit of addressing* it, rather than ignoring it? If you are asked "What is your *performance management system*?" do you have an answer?

Make sure you're staying positive, but also communicating specifically and immediately when something needs to be done differently (or at all!).

Make sure no one is lulled into false complacency because you're afraid to deal with consistent performance issues.

Even if it's informal, make sure there's a system – job descriptions, one-on-ones, daily or weekly "check-ins", TPS reports; something to keep an eye on the work. As Drucker says, "What gets measured, gets done."

Stay positive. Stay encouraging. Build real relationships. Meet needs. Then make sure the work gets done.

Rate yourself – and ask others to rate you – on this:

In the midst of building positive relationships, sticking to new habits, and seeking to meet needs, I do not let the <u>work</u> get neglected.

(low)   1   2   3   4   5   (high)

Self-perception:

_____

_____

_____

Feedback from others:

_____

_____

_____

_____

_____

SECTION EIGHT: PASSION

Positive Passion!

Leaders must have passion; that is, in their own way, they must show that they care.

Talk can only go so far – while an occasional well-done pep talk can be great with the right context and timing, it's what you *do* that demonstrates your passion. There's a lot you can do to show your passion and commitment. Some ideas:

Approach your duties with energy and determination. Affirm actions and projects that align with the values of the organization. Enforce high standards by providing timely, specific, behavior/outcome-based feedback. Only hire/bring on the absolute best fits for the organization.Actively and deliberately build your team – by working hard together. On occasion, do the "dirty work" and menial tasks that no one wants to do, but are absolutely necessary.

"Leadership is the art of mobilizing others to want to struggle for shared aspirations."

– Jim Kouzes and Barry Posner

Rate yourself – and ask others to rate you – on this:

If you ask the people I interact with, they will all tell you that I am passionate about our work.

(low)   1   2   3   4   5   (high)

Self-perception:

_____

_____

_____

Feedback from others:

_____

_____

_____

_____

_____

Reading 46

CHANGE THE PACE

I had a college professor who told us to "do everything 10% faster." This professor had lots of energy, and got lots done. And, the students who followed this advice seemed to work harder, have more energy, and be happier. Over the last 25 years this advice has proven invaluable; it works for me, too.

Not only does following this advice generate more productivity, more energy, and more happiness, it also provides a needed change of pace. When we change up our pace and alter our routine, we become more aware of our work and become more productive.

Sometimes life gets frantic. Dr. Lee's advice dates from the middle of last century, and technology has caused us to accelerate our pace and our frequency of communication. So, while this idea of moving faster still makes sense, another bit of advice might be helpful when we stress:

Sometimes, do everything 10% more slowly. Changing the pace downward–downshifting– can help us reflect more, de-stress, become less frantic, breathe more deeply, and have more fun.

Effective leaders will change up their pace, because they know it helps their energy and productivity. In fact, if you can't decide which direction you ought to change the pace, just pick one randomly. Just the change will help you reflect on whether or not it was a good idea.

Changing up your pace will help you get more done, have more energy, and enjoy life more. Give it a shot.

Rate yourself – and ask others to rate you – on this:

I periodically call for a change of pace - from myself or from others - to amp up energy and productivity, or reflect and de-stress.

(low)   1   2   3   4   5   (high)

Self-perception:

_____

_____

_____

Feedback from others:

_____

_____

_____

_____

_____

Reading 47

● ● ●

SEND HANDWRITTEN NOTES TO YOUR PEOPLE

When I was a teacher, I didn't get a lot of handwritten notes from my principals and superintendents.

So when I did, it was pretty exciting...

I once opened a note from my boss that appeared in my work mail slot without warning or fanfare. There was no significant event that precipitated it; she just wrote "You may not realize this, but your leadership in your department is noticed, and appreciated, and gives me ideas about what other departments are capable of."

To think that my boss would make the time to write words of appreciation or encouragement when a pop-by or email might have sufficed, really made a major impression and boosted my morale.

And, I bet that the act of writing the note made *her* feel better as well.

I once sent a handwritten not to a former colleague, thanking him for his informal mentorship and giving a couple of examples of how it was affecting my current practice. He responded by calling me, and we reconnected.

We both felt great, and motivated, and the act of writing and sending the note consumed fewer than five minutes.

Put a reminder in your calendar every, say, three weeks to pick a direct report — or even a peer — to write a note to.

It will boost you, and them, and remind them that you notice and appreciate their work.

Rate yourself – and ask others to rate you – on this:

I send handwritten notes of thanks and praise to my team members.

(low)   1   2   3   4   5   (high)

Self-perception:

_____

_____

_____

Feedback from others:

_____

_____

_____

_____

_____

Reading 48

ALIGN WORK WITH VALUES

Earlier, we talked about rubrics in general as a tool to develop vision. Let's take that further to talk about a way to make your passion more obvious to your team.

Examine all your own projects, initiatives, to-do items, daily tasks, and responsibilities. Compare each of them to your organizational values. Consider eliminating or delegating the ones that are needed, but are less aligned with your values. This is a way to focus your work AND develop your people.

Then, make sure the initiatives and tasks that align best with your vision and values are the ones you talk about, execute with vigor, and turn into object lessons.

For example, if your team values creativity and innovation, consider outsourcing filing compliance reports and inventory crosschecks. At the same time, make brainstorming sessions a priority, hold them in an obvious space, and be sure to follow-through on the best ideas.

Lastly, turn that process into a story of success at a staff meeting. Meanwhile, stop reporting about routine processes at meetings, and just deal with those things via email.

Align your work with your values, then share success stories to show your passion for the work.

Rate yourself – and ask others to rate you – on this:

I check regularly to make sure my work is aligned with my organization's values.

(low)   1   2   3   4   5   (high)

Self-perception:

_____

_____

_____

Feedback from others:

_____

_____

_____

_____

Reading 49

● ● ●

SPREAD PASSION WITH TESTIMONIALS

The marketing value of client or customer testimonials is clear, but let's talk about other reasons to gather and share them:

- They help you spread your passion.
- They help you keep the members of your team fired up.
- They keep you and your team ever-mindful of their purpose.

I had a great vet once who worked miracles for my cat. I wrote a letter to him, and told him he could use it in any way he wanted. While he did put excerpts on his website, he also framed the letter and put it in back, away from pet owners, but in daily full view for himself and his staff.

"Keeps us reminded why we do what we do," he said.

A client once reported a life-changing breakthrough as a result of some DiSC® training I provided. While it would work great as a marketing tool, it was too detailed to make public. I did, with permission, share it with a team leader in Product Development who works with DiSC, and she responded with this: "…thanks again for sharing this story. I was wondering if you would mind if

I shared it with my team – sometimes we become a little distanced from the effects of this work that we do, and I think they would really appreciate this tangible evidence of the power of the products."

So, are you accumulating testimonials? Or, have you avoided them, because business is good enough and you don't need them for marketing, or because they're too "braggy" and that goes against your grain?

Gather them anyway, to use internally.

This is one way to stay passionate, and remind your people why their work makes a difference.

Rate yourself – and ask others to rate you – on this:

I gather and keep testimonials posted in the workplace to keep my team fired up and ever mindful of our purpose.

(low)   1   2   3   4   5   (high)

Self-perception:

_____

_____

_____

Feedback from others:

_____

_____

_____

_____

_____

Reading 50

USE CASE STUDIES

Testimonials can be powerful tools for keeping that spark of passion alive in your workplace.

What if you don't have testimonials?

Write your own!

Think back on some of your greatest successes – the things that motivate you and your team to keep coming back.

If your client or customer didn't provide a testimonial, you can create your own.

You can turn it into a "case study," by putting into writing the high points of your work and the difference it made.

Or, you can just use "before and after" snapshots (if it's visual) or brief descriptions of the before and after.

Here are a few examples:

1. Our house is being painted. We're happy with the work, but aren't likely to write a testimonial. The crew leader could, however, take a before picture, and an after picture of their work. The pictures could then be posted back at the office to remind the team of their great work.
2. I know a dentist who takes before and after pictures of some severe cases. Those aren't always pretty for public consumption, but the staff can see them in the lab and be reminded of how much better teeth can make life more pleasant.
3. In the early days of my business, I had an economic development coordinator interview me, and a couple of clients, and write up some case studies. Organizations that support small businesses or economic development may have staff people who are available for this kind of service.

Going through this work yields two benefits:

1. You may end up with some decent marketing material.
2. You now have another way to show your passion to your team, and remind them of the importance of their work.

Rate yourself – and ask others to rate you – on this:

I use (or create) case studies to help motivate and spread passion for our work.

(low)   1   2   3   4   5   (high)

Self-perception:

_____

_____

_____

Feedback from others:

_____

_____

_____

_____

_____

NUMBER 51

Remember my mistaken assumption from the beginning?

"The last thing the world needs is another book on leadership."

I was wrong to resist the call to action and the push to provide this book. I hope it's been helpful, of course. But I still say

"There are plenty of books on leadership."

So what's not in this book? What's something you've learned somewhere else, that you know is essential for your leadership journey?

Record it here:

_____

_____

_____

_____

_____

Create your own summary of this behavior at the top of the next page.

Rate yourself – and ask others to rate you – on this:

_____

_____

_____

(low)   1   2   3   4   5   (high)

Self-perception:

_____

_____

_____

Feedback from others:

_____

_____

_____

_____

Now go meet needs. Start now.
Thanks for reading,

Alan Feirer

REFERENCES

Arbinger Institute (2000). *Leadership and self-deception: Getting out of the box.* San Francisco, CA: Berrett-Koehler.

Block, P. (1993). *Stewardship: Choosing service over self-interest.* San Francisco, CA: Berrett-Koehler.

Carnegie, D. (1964). *How to win friends and influence people.* New York, NY: Simon and Schuster.

Collins, J. C. (2001). *Good to Great: Why some companies make the leap--and others don't.* New York, NY: Harper Business.

Disney Institute., & Kinni, T. (2011). *Be our guest: Perfecting the art of customer service.* White Plains, NY: Disney Publishing.

Greenleaf, R. K. (1991). *The servant as leader.* Indianapolis, IN: Robert K. Greenleaf Center.

Heifetz, R. A., & Linsky, M. (2002). *Leadership on the line: Staying alive through the dangers of leading.* Boston, MA: Harvard Business School Press.

Horstman, M., & Auzenne, M. *Become a Better Manager and Have a More Successful Career.* Retrieved from http://www.managertools.com/

Kouzes, J. M., & Posner, B. Z. (1993). *Credibility: How leaders gain and lose it, why people demand it.* San Francisco, CA: Jossey-Bass.

Kouzes, J. M., & Posner, B. Z. (1995). *The leadership challenge: How to keep getting extraordinary things done in organizations.* San Francisco, CA: Jossey-Bass.

Lautzenheiser, T. (1992). *The art of successful teaching: A blend of content & context.* Chicago, IL: GIA Publications.

Pink, Daniel H. (2009). *Drive: The surprising truth about what motivates us.* New York, NY: Riverhead Books.

Ury, William (2007). *The power of a positive no: Save the deal save the relationship and still say no.* New York, NY: Bantam Books.

Walter, Jr. Wangerin (1984). *Ragman: and other cries of faith.* New York, NY: Harper & Row.

Welch, Jack, Welch, Suzy. (2005) *Winning.* New York, NY: Harper Business.

ACKNOWLEDGEMENTS...

My wife, editor, and business partner, Julie Feirer, did most of the initial editing, and final editing, and some detail work.

Ashleigh Rader, our assistant, did most of the detail work on the formatting and rearranging, and did a lot of editing, and catching little things, and putting up with me changing my mind about stuff a lot.

Jordan Kuhns designed the cover, with input from Jay Ewart, and has done the work of getting to know my brand and infuses it nicely in his graphics work for Group Dynamic. Jordan also executed the final layout and formatting to prepare this book for publication.

Matt Pries has proofread and provided feedback for much of my writing and oral delivery over the last several years, and this book was no exception. He's a great advocate, and fine writer, speaker, and leader in his own right.

Cecelia Munzenmaier has always been generous with feedback and wisdom.

Samantha Boyd ghostwrote some blogs for me a while back, and some of that content appears here.

Dr. Tim Lautzenheiser has assimilated so much work on motivation and leadership, and when I asked him once how he felt about me "stealing" some of his "stuff," he responded with "Is it being used to *build people?* If so, then *steal away!*" Done, sir. The Four Levels of Maturity have taken on a life of their own.

ABOUT GROUP DYNAMIC...

Group Dynamic sessions are designed to help leaders and teams get more done with less stress and interference. Learn more at **www.groupdynamic. net**. While my work as a teacher, and as Group Dynamic, has helped thousands learn about the concepts in this book, it is also true that I have learned much from all of my clients and students, and they have shaped me and the content. All solutions are a temporary resting place.

AFTERWORD

THE VIEW FROM ROCK BOTTOM

This is how Group Dynamic and my career in leadership training and development began.

It wasn't pretty.

The year was 1996, and I was despondent and irritated while I was at work, pretty much all of the time. I was in a well-earned and long-sought after position of leadership, a great job by any measure, but "my people" weren't engaged. They didn't get me. They weren't loyal. They weren't receptive, they weren't performing up to par, and they were leaving me. It wasn't *my* fault, of course... They just needed more time to get to know me! Right?

Except... there were signs to the contrary.

My boss said, on several occasions, "They are fighting you," but instead of considering his comment thoughtfully, I dismissed him as paternalistic.

My colleague raged, in a moment when I'd pushed her a little too far, "They are tired of you acting like you're their *king!*" Geez, I thought. She must be jealous! I still didn't get it. I called my predecessor, Jim, to ask, "What's their problem? Why isn't this working??"

Jim knew the answer but was too diplomatic to hold up a mirror.

So, as any recent graduate with a master's degree might do, I turned to the books. Surely, research would tell me the answer. Thank goodness, the first thing I checked out of the library was *The Leadership Challenge* by Kouzes and Posner, and it quickly helped me diagnose what "their" problem was.

The problem was me. (I bet you saw that coming.)

SEEKING WISDOM FROM THE GIANTS

For a while after this revelation I was even more discouraged. But then, I started reading and digesting every relevant thing I could get my hands on. After *The Leadership Challenge* I read some other weighty stuff by Senge and Greenleaf, some popular titles by Pitino and McGinnis, Covey and Carnegie. I took notes, outlined, highlighted, and made charts to track the commonalities between these authors and their ideas.

It was rigorous in some ways, and most certainly nerdy, but it was also time well spent. Those notes, charts, and scribbles evolved into an 8-point leadership model that saved "my people" from me.

Passionate, motivated, and cheered by the success of that model, I began to share it with others in my first industry, education, as a curriculum. The response was overwhelmingly positive, and after about twelve years, that work became my full-time vocation in classrooms and board rooms around the Midwest and beyond.

This book is a supplement to that curriculum, an introduction to the 8-Point Leadership Model that provides the foundation of my work with others in leadership, training, and organizational development.

ART AND THE ORIGIN OF THE 8-POINT LEADERSHIP MODEL

Prior to writing this book, I searched for the handwritten matrix I used as my crude research guide during that period of heavy reading and weighing ideas, so I could share a picture of it here. I'm bummed that I can't find it! I remember it all coming down to a "Top 4" and a "Top 8" — that is, four tenets that were basically undisputed, and four more with wide support that also resonated with me.

The top four were: *Service, Vision, Integrity,* and *Communication.*

The other four were *Modeling, Stretching & Growing* (often called other things, like "Sharpening the Saw," or "Constant Self-Improvement"), *Positivity,* and *Passion.*

There were others that weren't universally identified as primary leadership traits, but rather behaviors, that seemed worthy of inclusion, such as "sharing the credit," "risk-taking," and "celebrating and encouraging."

At this point the content was shaping up but the format was unwieldy, and I realized I needed to get it organized. I needed help.

I called Art.

It's good to have someone in your life who can talk sense into you, to keep you humble while giving you support, to balance motivation with caution, and to stand above you on the balcony to give you the big picture.

For much of my college career, that was Art. He was caution to my impulse, calm to my hyper, and always let me make mix tapes from his eclectic CD collection. He was also our campaign manager when his girlfriend, Amy, and I ran for Student Body President/Vice-President. (We lost the election, but the two of them are now married with three awesome kids.)

Art was one of the absolute best "people" people I've ever known — and still is, by the way. His path led him to higher education, working in student life. He's a Dean of Students now.

He was, and is, a great leader. So, when I was getting all impulsive and motivated to cram this curriculum together into a content-laden, un-digestible "leadership feast," I knew that Art could help me streamline it into something that made sense. He said something like this:

"Scale it down to six elements, and make it a triangle. Three on the points, three on the sides. Six. Easy to picture, easy to remember, easy to use.

"But I have ELEVEN!" I argued.

"Scale it down to six."

"Can't do it."

"Yes you can."

"Fine. Eight! Service, Vision, Integrity, Communication, Modeling, Stretching & Growing, Positivity, and Passion."

"Nope, too many. You could make it seven, and put one in the middle..."

"I'll combine positivity and passion, and stick 'Positive Passion' in the middle."

"Fine. That's seven."

"Eight."

"Fine."

Art is a great friend, and an amazing man. And since 1998, thousands of people have experienced this curriculum, and filled in their triangles in their handout booklets. But they don't know Art's role. That's okay with him; he is the picture of humility and lives to serve, not get kudos. But isn't that the way it always is with folks like Art?

So – credit where credit is due. I don't know where Group Dynamic and this leadership curriculum would be if it weren't for Art Sunleaf.

This book outlined the Group Dynamic Leadership Model that was born of my own pursuit of a more successful and rewarding relationship with the people I worked with, and emerged through research, development, and my work with Art. I hope it did well at taking you through each point in the model, fleshing out the importance of each and ideas for their real-life application.

If so, thank Art, Kouzes, Posner, Lautzenheiser, Senge, McGinnis, Horstman, and all those other giants whose shoulders we stand on.

Made in the USA
Middletown, DE
16 February 2017